THE BIOGRAPHY

OF A

LEGAL DISPUTE

—————

An Introduction

to

American Civil Procedure

By

MARC A. FRANKLIN
Professor of Law, Stanford University

Mineola, New York
THE FOUNDATION PRESS
1968

Franklin '68 Pamph. FP
4th Reprint—1972

PREFACE

The legal process is one of the most fundamental yet least understood aspects of American government. This may be attributable to the fact that the courts, which have a major formative role in this process, are rarely given equal billing with the executive and legislative branches of government. This book is an effort to redress that imbalance.

We follow an actual lawsuit step by step from the occurrence that gave rise to it to the decision that concluded it. The dispute involves a suit for libel brought against a newspaper. This particular dispute has been selected for several reasons. It conveys much that is widely relevant to the entire civil law, it can be illustrated at each stage by the actual legal documents, and both the facts and the law of the case are part of everyday experience and can be grasped readily. This study focuses on the functions of the judiciary in the resolution of disputes, and also touches on such related matters as the adversary system, the role of the jury, and the impact of our federal system on the judicial process. An Appendix suggesting further reading follows the text.

All too often the law is veiled in mystery. This book is intended to enable the citizen to become more aware of the workings of the American judicial system, and particularly the role of our courts in resolving civil disputes.

MARC A. FRANKLIN

Portola Valley, California
June 29, 1968

ACKNOWLEDGMENTS

Several persons have contributed substantially to the preparation of this book. My colleagues Douglas Ayer and Jack Friedenthal helped me avoid pitfalls along the way; Timothy Flynn, a recent graduate of the Stanford School of Law, helped develop text material throughout; Messrs. Louis Lisman and John Mulvey facilitated my access to the records in the case; and Mrs. Margaret Ferguson continually provided patient and careful secretarial assistance.

Finally, excerpts from the quoted articles and books are reprinted with the kind permission of the following copyright holders:

> Frank, Jerome, Courts on Trial, (reprinted by permission of the Princeton University Press, © copyright 1949 by Jerome Frank);

> James, Fleming, Jr., Civil Procedure (Boston, Little, Brown and Co., 1965);

> Kalven, Harry, "The Dignity of the Civil Jury," Virginia Law Review, Vol. 50 (1964);

> Rostow, Eugene, "The Lawyer and His Client," American Bar Association Journal, Vol. 48 (1962).

TABLE OF CONTENTS

THE BIOGRAPHY OF A LEGAL DISPUTE— AN INTRODUCTION TO AMERICAN CIVIL PROCEDURE

TABLE OF CONTENTS

THE BIOGRAPHY OF
A LEGAL DISPUTE

A SUIT FOR LIBEL

A. A GRIEVANCE ARISES

Our law suit concerns Ronald W. Towle, who was, in 1957, a 36-year-old Air Force Sergeant. On May 28, 1941, he had been involved in an automobile accident in Vermont in which a passenger in his car was killed. Towle was adjudged guilty of careless and negligent operation of a motor vehicle and his right to operate a motor vehicle in the state of Vermont was suspended. To get his license reinstated Towle had to demonstrate that he was financially responsible. In 1946, after returning to Vermont from military service, Sgt. Towle acquired the necessary liability insurance and had his driver's license officially reinstated. Soon thereafter, however, Sgt. Towle moved to Virginia and allowed his Vermont automobile liability insurance to lapse. His Vermont license was therefore suspended again. While in Virginia, Sgt. Towle acquired a Virginia driver's license valid until 1958. His car was fully insured. In 1957 Sgt. Towle was back in Vermont but had not reinstated his Vermont driver's license.

On November 25, 1957, Sgt. Towle was arraigned in the Franklin County Municipal Court in St. Albans for driving on Vermont roads while his Vermont license was suspended. He pleaded guilty to that offense and paid the $50.00 fine plus $12.30 in court costs.

St. Albans (pop. 8,552) is a town in the northwestern corner of the state 13 miles from the Canadian border. Its local paper, the St. Albans Daily Messenger, was an evening paper with a circulation of 3,254. The town of Fairfax, Sgt. Towle's home (pop. 1,129), was about 12 miles south of St. Albans and had no newspaper. That evening the Messenger carried the following story on page 2.

2—THE DAILY MESSENGER, MONDAY, NOV. 25, 1957

Leaders

Continued from page 1

—Tunisian arms. The French are still angry over the "token" delivery of rifles and submachineguns to Tunisia by Britain and America.

—Algeria. France wants assurances of British support again this year when the Algerian crisis is debated in the United Nations. This may not be forthcoming; since Britain feels Gaillard's plans for Algeria are not sufficient to end the rebellion and that the rebellion threatens NATO.

—NATO. France claims that Britain and the United States plan to set up an Anglo-American "directorship" to run NATO. British Foreign Minister Selwyn Lloyd who accompanied Macmillan today has emphatically denied this.

Dr. Teller

(Continued from Page 1)

short time" ICBM's which are accurate enough to hit such American cities as Houston, Tex.

Sharp Warning

The Hungarian-born scientist, now associate director of the University of California radiation laboratory at Livermore, Calif., warned that unless the United States steps up its military missile program "there is no doubt that the Russians will leave us behind and way behind."

Under questioning by Special Counsel Edwin L. Weisl, Teller said continued testing of nuclear weapons is "absolutely necessary."

He said the United States has developed a "clean type bomb" which "is already effective in that it cuts out 95 per cent of radio-activity."

Great Significance

Teller said Russia's space satellites have "very great significance," both militarily and scientifically, because they show Russian technological progress.

He said the Russian Sputniks of themseves were not positive proof that the Soviets have he ICBM. But he said it would be a "great mistake to proceed under the assumption that they are only bluffing" in claiming to have developed the long-range missile.

He said it is "reasonable to believe" that the Russians, like the United States, have solved the re-entry problem— the means of getting a missile back through the earth's atmosphere without it burning up from friction.

Teller said U. S. ICBM planning was to develop an effective warhead first.

Without a warhead, the long-range missile would not be very effective," he added. "The lighter we can make these warheads, the easier the job of the missile man is."

The United States, he went on, fell behind Russia because it "waited too long" for the right king of warhead to be available.

"We did not go ahead with a vigorous program of long-range missiles before we were reasonably sure that a warhead was available," he

Arraign Nine In Municipal Court Today

Nine uersons were arraigned before Judge Carl S. Gregg in Franklin Municipal Court this morning.

Ronald Cross of Cambridge pleaded guilty of failure to stop for a stop sign. He was fined $10, and costs of $5.10.

The same charge, plea and fine were levied in the case of Frederick Whitehead of Montgomery.

Gerald Paradis of Enosburg costs of $5.10, after pleading guilty of failure to stop for a stop sign.

A plea of guilty to driving while under suspension brought a fine of $550 and costs of $7.59, plus a sentence of 10 days in Franklin County jail, to Vernon Garrett of Fairfax.

Ronald Towle of Fairfax, an air policeman, formerly of Enosburg, pleaded guilty to driving while intoxicated. He paid a fine of $50 and costs of cated. He paid a fine of $50 $12.30.

A man from Iberville, Que., Roland Champagne, pleaded guilty to driving while intoxi and costs of $12.30.

Howard Constantine, 16, of St. Albans, pleaded innocent to careless and negligent driving with accident resulting. He was released in $200 bail.

Lanny Rich, 22, of St. Albans, was released in $300 bail, after pleading innocent to a change of driving while under suspension.

A 16-year-old youth from St. Albans Town, Norman Leduc, pleaded guilty to violation of the law of the road. He was fined $5, plus costs of $6.70.

Deaths

(Continued from Page 1)

Lester, he was going to search for the downed plane Saturday. The World War 2 veteran was said to be in ill health and despondent.

defenses" and the steps that must be taken to meet the Soviet challenge.

Johnson said the subcommittee hoped to get a clear definition during its inquiry of the threat to U. S. security, which he described as "perhaps the greatest our country

Study

(Continued from Page 1)

11 government office of scientific research and development, were billed as the first witnesses as the subcommittee started its first round of hearings on U.S. missiles and space developments.

Others on the program today were Dr. John P. Hagen, director of Project Vanguard for launching the U.S. earth satellite, and Dr. John Chipman of Massachusetts Institute of Technology who recently visited Soviet research facilities.

Morrison

(Continued from Page 1)

added there has been no official comment so far.

Morrison is being eyed as the undisputed possibility for the Democratic gubernatorial nomination next year. However, he has yet to say whether or not he would accept. While he repeatedly indicates that he wouldn't, party leaders continue to hint that they have "inside information" to the contrary.

In scrutinizing the first report they say there is little likelihood that Morrison would run for governor without resigning as tax commissioner.

Concerning the second, they argue that Morrison — the man most feared by the GOP. Therefore, they say that giving him a seat on the superior court bench would remove the threat of his opposing Stafford next year.

Nixon

Continued from page 1

launching "a massive nonmilitary offensive aimed at the overthrow of all free nations." He predicted the dictators of Moscow will sharply step up their economic, psychological and subversive activities, they will emphasize again the popular front tactics which fooled so many well-intentioned people in times past."

Nixon warned this country must avoid panic which "can lead to hasty and ill-considered programs", and compla-

If you were Sgt. Towle would you be distressed by this story? How precisely can you identify the cause of your concern? Are you distressed by the fact that the article appeared in a newspaper? Would you care as much if the newspaper were a local newspaper that circulated only in some remote state? What would be your reaction if instead of printing this in a newspaper, the editor called you on the phone and read you the story?

Is part of your concern based on the falsity of the item? If so, would you be equally concerned if your age were falsely stated to be 42 instead of 36? Is the story as written more distressing than an accurate account would have been?

Should the legal system provide a remedy to Sgt. Towle in this kind of situation? If so, what kind of remedy do you think it should be? What alternatives come to mind?

On the next evening, the 26th, the following story appeared in the lower left hand quadrant of the Messenger's front page with a two column continuation at the top of page three.

Wednesday the last 225 troops of the 101st Airborne Division who made it possible, with bare and ready bayonets, for nine Negroes to attend Central High School.

The job of protecting the

Ex-Sheriffs' Patrolman Admits Count

A man who five months ago was suspended from the Franklin County Sheriffs' Patrol was arraigned in municipal court here yesterday, pleading guilty to driving for the past nine years on a suspended license.

Ronald Towle of Fairfax, who was dropped from the patrol in June for "misuse of authority," was brought before Municipal Court Judge Carl S. Gregg, and was fined $50, plus costs.

A sergeant with the Air Police at the St. Albans Air Force Base, the 36-year-old native of Enosburg had his license suspended by the commissioner of motor vhicles in 1948, after he failed to file automobile liability insurance while he was overseas in the Army.

State police said that Towle was convicted of careless and negligent driving, death resulting.

(See TOWLE, page 3)

enhower when he ordered in the paratroopers, but still residents of Arkansas.

Because of the Thanksgiving holidays, which begin Wednesday, the first possible test of the quality of protection of the National Guardsmen will come next Monday.

In command of the National Guardsmen is Maj. Gen. Edwin Walker, a regular Army officer and commander of the Arkansas military district.

Sees Violence

Gov. Orval Faubus does not think all the troops could leave now without violence.

"If I had to hazard a speculation, it would be that some federal force will have to remain at the school until the end of the term if the Negroes are still enrolled," Faubus said.

His phrase, "if the Negroes (See TROOPS, page 3)

Reaction Violent To Article Challenging Vermont Principles

MONTPELIER — (UP) — Violent reaction is being recorded in Vermont today both for and against an article describing the Green Mountain State as "full of baloney, hokum, Snobbery, hokum and guff."

In the (Harper's) magazine article, Miss Miriam Chapin, a sixth generation Vermonter, says "It's about time Vermonters came out from behind the maple sugar bush, out

from under the covered bridge, took off their patchwork quilts and looked themselves in the eye."

Among other charges, Miss Chapin says town elections are rigged, the poll tax is high and Vermont is a fief of Boston and New York.

When the article was made public native Vermonters and "outlanders" began to take sides.

Those who stoutly defended (See REACTION page 3)

Alert Jordan, Saudi Arabia Of 'Dangers'

By UNITED PRESS

Jordan's Ramallah Radio alerted Jordanian and Saudi Arabian troops today against "Zionist danger."

Armed Jordanian soldiers patrolled the streets of old Jerusalem throughout the night and this morning and the situation was reported quiet but tense.

There was no report on the activities of the Saudi Arabian troops who entered Jordan last year during Israel's invasion of the Sinai Peninsula.

Confirmed

(See MID-EAST, page 3)

tling against t
to win some
tish support
tional Assemb
Algerian Hom
in the day.

The rift in
ance develo
United State
flew token ar
Tunisia over I
They hoped t
sian arms to
feared the all
(See TAL

Red Sp Expecte Over V

BY UNIT

Scientists of had conflictin the actual dea nik I's rocket peared certai culations that minent.

British exp that the eart will crash to

The Sovie n said Monday t fall during th of December it would dis hitting the ea

Scienists at Astrophysical Cambridge, M time ago the probably fall 11."

Experts th said they bel would hit the the terrific s atmosphere.

Mo nadynihi

Monday nig moonwatch te rocket in the was schedulec more passes States today in the Norhea

WEA

Partly clou afternoon wit flurries, mai elevations. N quite cold to continued c morning follo ing cloudines noon.

Ghosts Of Long Dead Red Men, White Men Stirred In Modern Court In Land Battle

WASHINGTON — (UP) — Ghosts of long-dead red men and white men stirred in the modern courtroom.

The Seneca Indians were

fighting for some shreds of their primeval empire.

Once the Seneca ruled vast forests stretching across Western New York and Pennsylvania and far into Ohio. Settlement by settlement, white men occupied the land.

Case In Court

Federal District Judge John J. Sirica sat listening impassively Monday to the story of the Senecas and his country.

The government lawyer said the government was not breaking the old treaty by taking the land. Edward E. O.'-Neill, the Indians' lawyer, said the government could not take the land without breaking the treaty.

"If they want it, we can't stop them," he said. "But they must pass a special act abrogating the treaty. It's an Indian land grab."

The judge said he would study the case. He asked O'Neill if he would go to the Court of Claims if he lost the case in Federal District Court.

"I'll appeal," O'Neill said.

"It isn't money. If they take the land, that's all the Senecas have."

Towle

Continued from page 1

ing in St. Albans on May 19, 1941.

Troopers said a vehicle operated by him was involved in a fatal crash at Bakersfield. A passenger in the car was killed.

State police said he entered the armed service in 1943, and had his operator's license reinstated in 1946.

Two years later, troopers said Towle allowed his automobile liability insurance to lapse and his license was again suspended. Police said it has not been reinstated since.

In court yesterday, the former deputy reported having a Virginia license which is good for 4 years, and expires in 1958. Further, he said his car was fully insured.

Judge Gregg, meanwhile, said today court records show that as a deputy, the 36-year-old airman was the arresting officer in six motor vehicle cases prosecuted here during the months of May, June, and July.

As a deputy, Towle was given a permit by the commissioner of public safety to equip his car with a siren and red warning lights.

His appointment as a deputy sheriff was made by Franklin County Sheriff John R. Finn, and was approved by the Attorney —General of Vermont.

Finn said this morning his commission as deputy and his permit from the department of public safety were withdrawn when he was dropped from the patrol for misuse of authority and on order of the Office of Strategic Information, USAF., Ft. Ethan Allen, Vt.

President

(Continued from Page 1)

President's engagement with the king of Morocco. The meeting was held in the cabinet room of the White House.

Mrs. Wheaton gave no indication of just when the medical statement would be forthcoming this morning.

Given Sedation

The President developed the chill and was ordered to bed by his doctors after going to the Washington airport in chilly weather Monday to welcome the Moroccan king.

He was given mild sedation and slept comfortably through the night. The White House said Monday night he had no fever and that his pulse and respiration were normal.

It gave no specific word on what had caused the chill.

Mrs. Eisenhower and most of the White House staff did not appear to be alarmed, despite some White House speculation that the President may have come down with Asian flu. He received an Asian flu shot in August.

Talks

(Continued from Page 1)

against Macmillan on his ar-

Reaction

Continued from page 1

Vermont were mostly people who had moved here from other states. Some were quoted as saying "If Miss Chapin doesn't like it here she should move."

But native Vermonters seemed more in agreement with the article. One woman said "it's true town elections are rigged and some of the streams are filthy. But Miss Chapin must love Vermont enough to bring these things out."

Mid-East

(Continued from Page 1)

The Ramallah broadcast confirmed the troops were still in Jordan.

High Israeli sources predicted the crisis between Israel and Jordan might worsen within the next few days and expressed hope a visit by U. n. Secretary General Dag Hammarskjold would ease the situation.

Hammarskjold leaves New York Friday, and an Amman, Jordan, dispatch said he would arrive there Sunday in response to a cable from the government of King Hussein.

Beebes Attend IOOF Meeting

Mr. and Mrs. George Beebe of the Georgia road have returned from Worcester, Mass. where they attended a meeting of the Northeast Odd Fellow Association. Mr. Beebe is general chairman of the annual conclave of Northeast Odd Fellows, to be held in Barre, in June, 1958.

This includes Odd Fellows from the six New England states, the Province of Quebec, and the Maritime Provinces. Committee chairmen were named at this time.

On Saturday night, Mr. and Mrs. Beebe attended a reception in Montpelier in honor of Clyde Worthen, grand patriarch of the Grand Encampment of Vermont, Independent Order of Odd Fellows. They were accompanied on the entire trip by Mrs. Ruth Gage of Burlington, past president and present secretary of the International Association, Ladies' Auxiliary, Patriarchs Militant; and Miss Grace Norton of Burlington, Past President, Rebekah Assembly of Vermont.

Troops

(Continued from Page 17)

reach the Algerian rebels.

Youths Rioted

The anti-British feeling exploded into demonstrations are still enrolled," may spring from reports that the NAACP at mid-term will give the Negro children a choice of dropping out and attending a segregated school, or remaining.

This Mrs. L. C. Bates, president of the Arkansas Chapter of the NAACP, bitterly denies.

Tension Still Present

Under the surface, there is still plenty of tension in Little Rock. There are scattered reports of incidents between white students and the Negroes. School officials deny some and confirm others.

Principal J. W. Matthews appears annoyed because he figures the Army is "leaking" information about conditions in the school.

"It will be different when the Army leaves," he said.

City Briefs

Sati

(Continued fr significant".

research resu speech at Cleve

The display, l National Advisc for Aeronautic; amples of roc new types of en energy fuels to phasis on Ame catch up with tl The President have been sho

COMING

Notices of CO food sales rumn other fund rais cents for first th cents per line (after.

Novelty Part Holy Angels au Thursday nigh Parish sopnson Club.

Novelty party night, 7:30 p.m. Baptiste.

Novelty Part Parish Center, er, Vermont.] at 8 p.m.

Novelty Part day night at St. Club Rooms.

Novelty Party Moose Home, L Friday evening at

Novelty part day night 7:30 Hall 7 Lake St

Dancing Sa 8:45 p.m. 1 Jean Baptiste. Pee-Wee, Harr

Turkey Novel day, Nov. 25, b in B.F.A. Audit fax, benefit Church. 16 V pons and cash Prize and Free

Tuesday, No Card Party. School. 7:30 p.

$.50. Benefit I Novelty part nesday night ; Eagles Hall.

As we shall see, there is some vagueness about the "suspension" from the Sheriff's patrol for "misuse of authority." Assume now that that charge is false, and that Sgt. Towle had resigned from the patrol for unrelated reasons. Is this a more serious charge than the first publication? Why do you think the newspaper ran this story? Do you read this second story as having any bearing on the first story?

B. RETAINING AN ATTORNEY

After Sgt. Towle reads both stories and decides that he has a grievance what should he do? What would you do? Even such preliminary questions assume that if any legal action is to result from these newspaper reports it must be initiated by Sgt. Towle. This is one of the basic premises of our legal system. Similarly in criminal law, where the public interest as well as individual interests are involved, a government agent, the prosecutor or District Attorney, must decide whether to bring an alleged transgression before the court. Courts do not go out looking for business. At almost every stage some party must ask for relief or the court will remain a sleeping giant.

What are the reasons for this requirement? What are some of the consequences of leaving to the aggrieved the burden of going forward to vindicate his rights? On balance, is this burden desirable?

Once we accept the principle that the aggrieved party must do something, and that Sgt. Towle feels aggrieved, what should he do? It may be obvious to some that the Sergeant should see a lawyer to learn what rights he has. Recent studies show, however, that aggrieved persons occasionally handle their own cases, perhaps because they don't know how to find a lawyer or because of an unfortunate prior experience with the law.

As far as we know, Sgt. Towle was not represented by an attorney at the November 25th court session. Nor is there any indication that he had recently had one. How should he go about finding an attorney? Since attorneys are not permitted to advertise, Towle might ask a friend for a name, pick a name out of the phone directory or, perhaps, walk into a conveniently located law office. Shortly after the two newspaper articles, Sgt. Towle discussed his grievance with Mr. Louis Lisman of the firm of Lisman and Lisman in Burlington, Vermont, (pop. 33,-155) some 20 miles southwest of Fairfax and 28 miles south of

St. Albans. Mr. Lisman, born in 1910, attended the University of Vermont and earned his law degree at Harvard. He was admitted to the Vermont bar in 1935. We do not know how Sgt. Towle chose his attorney, but Mr. Lisman speculated that since he had a number of clients in Fairfax one of them had probably recommended him.

Sgt. Towle probably presented the facts as they appeared to him, emphasizing that he was a teetotaler and thus particularly resentful of the first publication about intoxication. He probably also expressed concern about a modest radio repair business he ran in his off-duty hours. It is unlikely that his facts were neatly organized in terms of legal relevance. It was up to his attorney to pick out the relevant facts and to ask questions to learn other facts that might not appear relevant to his client. Mr. Lisman quickly saw that Sgt. Towle's grievance was in the legal area called defamation. Since he did not specialize in defamation law, he may just have discussed superficially what Sgt. Towle's rights might be and what the problems might be. Perhaps Mr. Lisman raised a few problems peculiar to defamation, noting that if there were a trial it would draw attention to the 1941 accident as well as to the erroneous reports. Also, since harm to Sgt. Towle's reputation is the major issue in a case like this, it is appropriate for the defendant (the party being sued) to explore possible weaknesses in the plaintiff's (the complaining party's) reputation. Sgt. Towle could consider these problems while Mr. Lisman did some investigating on his own. Moreover, there would be inevitable problems of delay while Mr. Lisman worked on other matters and while this case was being prepared for trial should that prove necessary.

Defamation cases are often more complicated than are suits for breach of contract or automobile accidents. After the prospective client has told his story in a defamation situation serious questions may occur to the lawyer that he might not be ready to discuss with the client—such delicate questions as his client's general reputation in the locality before and after the defamation, and the possible truth of the charges. Mr. Lisman did not agree immediately to take Sgt. Towle's case. He wanted to do some investigation, and soon thereafter talked to over 30 people —townsfolk, servicemen, and others. In addition, from time to time Sgt. Towle brought letters from his radio repair customers that were harsh in their criticism of his alleged "driving-while-intoxicated."

As this indicates, an attorney who is consulted need not agree to represent the prospective client. One obvious reason for refusing a case is that it offers the attorney little or no prospect of remuneration. This matter will be considered shortly. Other reasons for refusal might be the subject matter of the case (some attorneys do not handle obscure legal areas with which they are unfamiliar) or an apparent personality conflict with the prospective client. Furthermore, some attorneys refuse to represent unpopular clients in any matter or to take unpopular cases. Reluctance to "get involved" and fear of economic, social, or political reprisal have caused many attorneys to shun cases. The following article excerpt discusses this problem.

————

THE LAWYER AND HIS CLIENT

Eugene V. Rostow

48 American Bar Association Journal 25, 27–30, 28 (1962).

Whatever the actual position was a century ago, today, in every community I know anything about, we have not lawyers only, as a single homogeneous group, but a complex hierarchy of lawyers: plaintiffs' lawyers and defendants' lawyers, men who represent insurance companies, and refuse all plaintiffs' cases, and those who live to prosecute tort claims. In the corporate field, lawyers who habitually defend stockholders' suits or antitrust cases often decline to bring them, on grounds of professional policy. The problem is the same in many other fields—labor law, for example, or the handling of malpractice cases. The men who represent publishers in libel cases are sometimes unavailable to those who wish to initiate such suits. In a few areas—taxation, admiralty and criminal law, for example—the link between the lawyer and his client's position is somewhat weaker, although even in criminal law it is hard to imagine some men with a reputation for the defense becoming district attorneys.

This feature of our professional life has given rise to grave concern throughout our history, when lawyers hesitated to accept clients who were violently unpopular, or were involved in controversies which aroused strong hostile feelings. John Adams defending the British soldiers in Boston; William H. Seward establishing the defense of insanity against a charge of murder; Clarence Darrow and Arthur Garfield Hays in some of their adventures at the Bar; Whitney North Seymour in the Herndon case; and many like episodes are part of our professional memory, and of our professional pride. But the problem symbolized by these great moments persists, in the difficulty the Bar has faced in recent years in providing counsel of the highest professional standing in many controversies over civil rights—those stemming from the enforcement of the Smith Act, for example; those arising out of the loyalty-security programs of the national and state governments; and the cycle of cases asserting the rights of Negroes under the Fourteenth Amendment. Cases of this order, where the legal process confronts an inflamed public opinion and challenges social habits with deep roots, provide the ultimate moral test of our profession and of the law. The troublesome questions such controversies present go beyond the issue of providing an adequate defense for the legal rights of unpopular defendants. They raise queries about the genuineness of our professional independence—questions which touch and color every aspect of our professional performance. I know we should all agree that without independent lawyers, capable of asserting the claims of the law in the courtroom without fear of reprisal, our legal system cannot be true to itself, and cannot hope in the long run to meet its basic social duties. I think we should equally agree that in the less dramatic affairs of the everyday world, the lawyer is not really a lawyer in advising a client about a contract, a will, or a merger, unless he can freely insist on the professional position he regards as right, in the accommodation of his client's interests to the law, even if the client doesn't like it. In the delicate equilibrium between the lawyer's duty to his client, and his duty to the law, every device for protecting the lawyer's professional integrity is worth careful consideration, for much is at stake. The real problem, as I see it, is whether lawyers represent the law as officers of the court, or whether they are no more than paid agents for the interests and preconceptions of their regular and expected clients.

The prevailing view in Britain provides a useful starting point for analysis.

It is of course commonplace that the profession of law with us is organized quite differently from the dual system of solicitors and barristers which flourishes in England, and that our Bar, by and large, is less unified, less controlled, and far more loosely organized than the profession in Britain.

[The essence of the English categories finds the solicitor performing all the functions of an American lawyer except that he may not appear in any of the major courts. The barrister is a specialist in advocacy who handles trials and appeals in these major courts. He may also be a specialist in a particular legal area and may be consulted on these matters. The barrister is distinguished from a successful American advocate by the convention that barristers do not have direct access to the lay client. Clients go to the solicitor, who may give general advice and handle cases in the lowest courts. If, however, major litigation is involved or if the solicitor wants a specialist's advice, it is he who will retain a barrister.—Ed.]

We and the British are alike in our general views of the law, in our methods of trial and adjudication, in our stubborn notion that the law protects the individual not only against other persons, but against the state as well. Unlike many other peoples, both we and the British take an incurably sporting view of litigation, which generations of procedural reformers have been unable entirely to destroy, and we both cherish rules which give the under-dog a fighting chance. Our judges, like theirs, are encouraged to write opinions in the form of personal essays, in an ancient fashion which lawyers trained in other traditions can never quite accept or understand. And both we and the British believe that an independent Bar is as vital to the rule of law as an independent judiciary. It is our common conviction that the legal process, conducted by independent judges, will be incapable of resisting public or private tyranny unless the judges are aided in the course of trials, and in all other aspects of the work of the profession, by equally independent lawyers, who have been schooled to provide a fearless and intransigent enquiry into every relevant circumstance of the problem being dealt with. We take it for granted, in our trials of Soviet spies or Japanese generals, that the lawyers for the defense should press every factual and legal issue to the limits of proper advocacy, as the British do—for example, in the trials of Roger Casement or Lord Haw-Haw. . . .

. . .

For the British, the ultimate guarantee of the independence of the Bar in all its functions—the accepted symbol of its professional detachment—is the rule that a barrister is bound to accept any brief in the courts in which he professes to practice. Normally, but not in cases of great public moment, the barrister can refuse a brief only if the fee offered is not properly professional, in view of the length and difficulty of the case. Otherwise, he can decline a brief only under special circumstances of conflict of interest, embarrassment, and the like.

. . .

The idea was pungently stated by Mr. Justice Neville in 1913: "As it once was put to me, always remember that you are in the position of a cabman on the rank, bound to answer to the first hail." The principle is alive in British practice, and is regarded there as an indispensable bulwark of personal liberty, and a vital protection for the integrity of the profession. Ingrained in the public mind, accepted by public opinion as the order of nature, this doctrine more than any other keeps lawyers in Britain at one remove from their clients, as a group apart, and makes it impossible to imagine a situation in that country in which lawyers are long identified with their clients' views, or criticized or penalized for providing them with professional services. I don't mean to suggest that lawyers in England are more popular than they are elsewhere, or that they are greatly loved. In England, as in every other country, the old suspicion persists, in Swift's famous words, that lawyers are men bred in the art of proving "that white is black and black is white, according as they are paid". But what I do mean is that in England, under the protection of the "cab rank" rule, the Bar can perform its basic task of representation or counsel on a stiffly professional and independent footing, without the restrictive influence of reprisal or penalty, and without becoming permanently identified with the views or status of any one client or class of clients. The barrister is much more closely linked to the law and to the courts than to his clients.

The code of ethics of the American Bar has never accepted the British rule in its full majesty, even in criminal cases. Canon 31 of the Canons of Professional Ethics adopted by the American Bar Association declares that "no lawyer is obliged to act either as adviser or advocate for every person who may wish to become his client. He has the right to decline employment." The Canon stresses the lawyer's individual responsibility for accepting or declining requests for professional services. And it makes no reference, directly or indirectly, to the principle of the English rule as a factor the lawyer is to take into account in exercising his responsibility. It should be added, however, that the lawyer's oath, recommended by the American Bar Association, and widely used, contains these words: "I will never reject, from any consideration personal to myself, the cause of the defenseless or oppressed." . . .

Despite the basic similarities of the law and the legal profession in Britain and the United States, there are fundamental differences as well. . . . In the realm of business and governmental affairs, our lawyers normally play a far more active role in the formation of policy than their British counterparts. . . . Many of the business policy services provided for corporate clients in this country by lawyers are supplied in England by accountants. We regard it as sound and desirable professional practice for a corporate lawyer to be continuously familiar with his client's business problems, and to participate in the shaping of his policies. It is common in the United States for lawyers to be directors of their corporate clients, although the professional wisdom of the practice has been questioned. . . .

More generally, the role of lawyers in our public and private affairs is far larger than that of the profession in Britain. . . . We live under a constitution which frequently requires lawyers to advise, and judges to decide, on the boundaries of governmental power. We live in a federal system which has in modern times developed formidable habits of regulation, and generates legal problems unknown in Britain, so that with us major business transactions are almost never undertaken, and should not be undertaken, save on advice of counsel. These features of our public life have given the law, the courts and the Bar a set of functions, and a place in the political process quite different from those which prevail in Britain. . . .

. . . I should suggest that the sustained responsibilities of many American lawyers for the policy problems of their clients, especially in business, labor and government, would make the British rule unworkable, and probably undesirable among us, for the larger part of the profession. Responsibilities of this order, implicit in the political system of the United States, and the extraordinary importance of the legal element in the process of making policy decisions throughout our society, can best be discharged by counsel who are thoroughly familiar with the factual realities of their client's position, without losing their professional detachment and freedom of maneuver.

On the other hand, the American Bar has long felt uneasy about its departure from the British rule. Many of our greatest men, especially among our trial lawyers, have sought to live by it. We have tried to preserve the essential idea behind the British rule, and to achieve its goals by other means. Thus the Bar has acknowledged, as a part of its uncodified tradition, the obligation "to see that all defendants, however unpopular, have the benefit of counsel for their defense." . . . Courts and bar associations pay deference to the principle, but it is still too often honored in the breach. . . .

One may agree with Rostow that the barrister's obligations and the American tendency to identify lawyers with their clients both tend to make the English bar more independent and professional than the American bar. On the other hand the British experience includes none of the harrowing domestic crises of the civil rights movement or the post-World War II civil liberties tensions—and it is here that the American bar has failed to demonstrate responsibility. In both countries outstanding attorneys have been willing to represent accused Nazi war criminals and accused Soviet spies, but ironically in the United States this same professional detachment has not extended to Negroes and civil rights workers in the South or to left wing ideologists in the North. The rise of organizations devoted to legal representation of some of these groups may be directly traced to the reluctance of individual attorneys to "become involved" in unpopular causes.

Our earlier observations about why the claimant has the initiative assumed that all who had grievances could obtain the services of an attorney, since very few citizens either attempt to, or are capable of, handling their grievances without an attorney. Dean Rostow's article, however, indicates that some unpopular persons may have difficulty obtaining legal assistance. Have you ever heard your friends or family condemn an attorney for taking an unpopular case? What are their grounds? Do they condemn a physician who treats an unpopular person? Or the butcher who sells him meat? Is an attorney any different?

Are physicians required to undertake the care of anyone who requests their services? What about a physician who witnesses a serious auto crash? Should our legal system force physicians to treat all who need their services? Should lawyers be compelled to accept all would-be clients? In which situation is selectivity more important?

One common question is how in a criminal case an attorney can accept a client whom he knows to be guilty. This very important matter may be approached on several levels. The adversary system, by which each party presents his own case and attacks his opponent's case, is thought to be the best method for deciding who has the stronger case. The attorney is not concerned with the guilt of his client; he resembles the English barrister who serves as the legal champion for anyone who wishes to retain him.

That role is especially important when the state seeks to punish a citizen. Here the lawyer is needed to protect the individual against the massive power of the state and to guarantee the citizen his rights in the courtroom. The prosecutor must try to prove guilt according to established ground rules; he may not, for instance, use evidence obtained illegally. Who is to make sure that the parties follow these procedures? Some think the judge himself could protect the defendant, but others answer that the quest for justice requires a clear division of function between the judge and the lawyer—and that the judge's decisions will not appear to be objective unless he has remained detached and impartial throughout the proceedings.

If these explanations of the role of the lawyer do not suffice, there are two further considerations. First, when a man is found guilty, there remains the matter of how severely he should be punished—and legal counsel is valuable here. Second, even if a lawyer were concerned with his client's guilt or innocence, how would he ever "know" whether his client was guilty?

Lawyers are sometimes condemned for making arguments in court that they do not consider stronger than those of their adversary. How might someone who thought that lawyers and judges should play distinctive institutional roles respond to this charge? In terms of Jonathan Swift's criticisms, whose function is it to decide what is black and what is white?

Another common concern about lawyers is that they thwart "justice" by finding "loopholes" in the law by which guilty parties escape punishment. In light of the role analysis just discussed, how might this matter be approached? What do most critics have in mind when they use the term "loophole?" The inscription above the entrance to the Supreme Court building in Washington, D. C. reads "Equal Justice Under Law." What does this mean? Is it relevant to the "loophole" situation?

We shall discuss later some of the complications that arise when, in the adversary system, the legal representation available to the opposing sides is of unequal quality.

Once Mr. Lisman has decided to take the case, how should he be compensated for his services? In deciding to consult a lawyer Sgt. Towle presumably considered the costs of doing so in a general sense, and his early discussions with Mr. Lisman may well have included some mention of a fee. Most lawyers commonly establish a fee reflecting the amount of time the case will require and also the type of legal work entailed. This basic rate would govern situations outside the courtroom such as drafting a will, preparing a contract, setting up a corporation or giving general advice on a legal problem. When litigation is involved, however, the basic hourly rate is affected by the outcome.

There is one major exception to this time-work fee computation: in this country virtually all lawyers in civil suits to recover damages for personal injuries charge a contingent fee. This provides that if there is a recovery the attorney receives a percentage of it; if the suit fails he receives no fee at all. The percentage is generally between 25% and 35%, though it may be higher if much work is involved and lower if the money is recovered easily. This enables injured parties to have legal counsel that they might not otherwise be able to afford. Before the Industrial Revolution only the wealthy were involved in civil law-suits. Since then, however, the urban and industrial environment has exposed the less wealthy to injuries for which others are liable and the contingent fee has enabled the victims to seek redress without government intervention. In most other countries the contingent fee is illegal or unethical because it involves the attorney deeply in the outcome of the case and might encourage him to engage in dubious tactics for his own financial gain. Indeed, claims of fee abuses seem to arise almost entirely out of the contingent fee arrangement rather than from the base rate arrangement. Does the contingent fee offend you?

In view of the limited applicability of the contingent fee, and our social commitment to justice for all, other means were needed to keep the courts open to all. Although many lawyers will handle an occasional case without any fee, public and private legal aid "clinics" more commonly handle cases for those unable to pay. Recent social legislation has made legal services available to the poor for civil suits and non-litigation advice in addition to previous access to counsel for indigent criminal defendants. One particularly important aspect is the availability of legal services for divorce matters. Since a divorce action by a poor person cannot possibly yield the kind of large award that may come from a personal injury suit there is no room for the contingent fee and thus no way in which a lawyer can be compensated. Without either free private representation or government-supplied legal services, divorces would be available only to those with money to pay legal fees and the family patterns of those at the other end of the economic spectrum could not possibly comport with the law's demands.

In the light of Sgt. Towle's limited financial resources, he and Mr. Lisman agreed upon a contingent fee for the handling of this case.

C. IDENTIFYING THE RELEVANT LAW

You will recall that Mr. Lisman did some interviewing and field investigating to assess the strength of Sgt. Towle's case and how closely the Sergeant's perceptions comported with those of his neighbors. But at the same time Mr. Lisman was also researching the legal consequences of these facts. He was not a specialist in defamation law but was what would be called in medicine a general practitioner. A well-trained general lawyer should be able to master an uncommon problem in most fields after some study. Mr. Lisman did not know all the technical rules of defamation and he was concerned about the legal implications of the fact that Sgt. Towle had indeed pleaded guilty to a traffic offense on November 25, although not the one the newspaper had reported.

To answer this and similar questions Mr. Lisman had to consult the "law". But whose law? In a country in which there is only one sovereignty to make rules the answer is simple. But in the United States, with its federal structure, the answer is sometimes complicated. Should Mr. Lisman research state law or is this a matter for federal law? Laymen sense this distinction in recognizing, for example, that questions involving military service are matters of federal law, while traffic violations and divorces are matters of state law. All efforts/to derive some general principles about the relationship between these two legal systems must start with the Constitution of the United States—our basic political document.

In the first three articles, Congress, the Executive, and the Judiciary, respectively, are given certain enumerated powers. But the fact that the federal government has been given certain powers does not necessarily mean that these powers are barred to the states. It is only when the laws of the two governments would conflict that the state law must give way. This result is ordained by the so-called supremacy clause of the federal Constitution, Article VI, Section 2:

> This Constitution, and the laws of the United States which shall be made in pursuance thereof; and all treaties made, or which shall be made, under the authority of the United States, shall be the supreme law of the land; and the judges in every State shall be bound thereby, anything in the Constitution or laws of any State to the contrary notwithstanding.

Determining the existence of a "conflict" so as to invoke the supremacy clause is a delicate constitutional problem. For now, we need only observe that since the Constitution delegates no power concerning private defamation to Congress or the Executive branch, there are no statutes on the subject and the problem does not arise.

The next question is what happens when there is no federal enactment? May the state do anything it wishes? Again, recourse to the federal Constitution is necessary—this time to the tenth amendment which provides that the "powers not delegated to the United States by the Constitution or prohibited by it to the states, are reserved to the states respectively, or to the people". The negative implications of the Tenth Amendment suggest another limitation on state action: powers the Constitution *prohibits* to the states. The prohibitions fall into two major categories. First, Article I, Section 10 forbids states to do such things as coining money, granting titles of nobility, and impairing the obligations of contract. Other state actions such as compacts between states are permitted only with Congressional consent. The second major group of activities prohibited to the states arises out of the post-Civil War 13th, 14th and 15th Amendments, which forbade slavery and voting discrimination and, more generally in the 14th Amendment, declared that no state shall "deprive any person of life, liberty, or property without due process of law; nor deny to any person within its jurisdiction the equal protection of the laws."

When Mr. Lisman investigated this sequence of questions, he quickly realized that no federal power was involved. Nor did he find anything in the Constitution prohibiting states from dealing with this case nor, we shall assume, was "due process" or "equal protection of the laws" relevant to the case.

Once it becomes clear that state law controls, the next question is which state? In Sgt. Towle's case the law must be that of Vermont because everything took place in Vermont. In other cases, this question is complicated. An example may make this clear. A man in New York may make a contract to sell goods being made in Illinois to a California buyer with delivery of the goods at the buyer's Texas plant. Which state's law will control if a dispute arises over the interpretation of that contract? If the law in all states is the same the question need not be faced. Often, however, the laws differ and the determination of which state's law to use will be crucial. When Mr. Lisman decided that state law controlled Sgt. Towle's case he could be confident that it was Vermont law.

D.   RESEARCHING THE LAW

Once Mr. Lisman decides which state's law applies, what does he do? The "law" of the State of Vermont has many sources. It may be found in the constitution of the State of Vermont, the state legislature's enactments (statutes), in regulations promulgated by state administrative bodies or in the decisions of its judiciary. The amount of research necessary would depend on Mr. Lisman's familiarity with the subject area. He would quickly find that his state constitution contained nothing relevant to this case and his basic knowledge of administrative law would tell him no regulations covered defamation. Agencies function in areas of public concern as evidenced by the Department of Motor Vehicles and the Alcoholic Beverage Commission. Thus Mr. Lisman would concentrate on statutory law and judicial decisions.

The statutes of Vermont are compiled by subject matter and are well indexed. Closely related sections are grouped in "titles." Each year's new statutes are added to the books by supplemental pamphlets. The statute books are often "annotated," which means that following each statutory provision the text will list all cases in which judges have discussed the particular provision. No lawyer can keep in mind the total content of his state's statutory provisions and we can be sure that Mr. Lisman looked for a statute that might be relevant to his case.

At this point we might note one statute that is relevant in every case—the statute of limitation. Mr. Lisman had no such concern because of Sgt. Towle's immediate resort to a lawyer, but suppose these events had occurred ten years ago and Sgt. Towle had just decided that he wanted to do something about it. All legal systems are concerned about stale claims; as time passes memories fade, evidence is lost, witnesses die or cannot be traced. Prospective defendants should not have to remain indefinitely in dread of being sued. On the other hand, the rules should not force those aggrieved to reach decisions hastily. The result has been a series of "statutes of limitation" in which aggrieved parties are required to initiate legal action within varying periods of time. The statute that Mr. Lisman found relevant was 12 V.S. § 512 (section 512 of Title 12, "Court Procedure," of the Vermont Statutes) providing that "Actions for the following causes shall be commenced within three years after the cause of action accrues, and not after: . . . (3) slander and libel; . . ." As we shall see, slander and libel are two subdivisions of defamation. Mr. Lisman now realizes that he has ample time to research and study this case before he must reach a final decision about suing.

As Mr. Lisman did his research he may have been especially concerned about one particular kind of statute. He may have been aware that several states have "retraction" statutes that require anyone who claims to have been defamed by a newspaper to write to the newspaper giving the details and demanding a retraction. In California, for example, this must be done "within 20 days after knowledge of the publication." Failure to comply, though not barring the plaintiff's action, does sharply curtail the amount of recoverable damages. A careful study of the Vermont statutes reveals no comparable statute nor any other relevant statute.

Finding no guidance elsewhere Mr. Lisman would conclude that the matter before him is controlled exclusively by judicial decisions. Some of our law has developed without legislative or constitutional influence. One party sensed a grievance against another and resorted to a court and demanded "justice." The courts searched the statute books to see if the case was covered there. If so, the court applied the statute to the case. If not, the court decided whether *it*, the court, should rule for the complainant. If it decided to do so, it would explain its reason in an opinion. Later courts confronted with the same or a similar problem might then have the benefit of the thinking of their predecessors on the question. The important point for present purposes is that such a body of law exists and controls Sgt. Towle's case.

Again there are research techniques and books available to help Mr. Lisman find the relevant Vermont cases. There are general legal encyclopedias that attempt to sketch broadly the law of defamation and also to review relevant cases in each state of the Union. If Mr. Lisman knows which specific problems he wants to research, he can by-pass the encyclopedias and rely on specially indexed materials to lead him to whichever Vermont cases discuss his problem. Remember, for example, Mr. Lisman's concern about the relevance of the fact that Sgt. Towle had actually been convicted of driving while under suspension. Recalling that truth is a complete defense to any claim for defamation, Mr. Lisman wondered whether the conviction would weaken or destroy any defamation action based on a false charge of driving while intoxicated. Mr. Lisman probably used one of several volumes searching for Vermont cases indexed under "truth"—or "justification" as it is sometimes called—within the more general topic of "defamation." There he would find a reference to an 1838 case in the Supreme Court of Vermont entitled Torrey v. Field, which was similar in that the defendant was unable to prove the truth of his statement but did assert the truth of a different charge. The court's opinion in that case contained the following language:

> The authorities all concur in this, that where the defendant will justify by showing the truth of the matters charged in the libel, it must be the truth of the "very

charge," and it is not sufficient to plead and prove the plaintiff guilty of a similar offense, or even of one more flagrant.

Having found this favorable precedent Mr. Lisman read all the other cases referred to. He then traced all the later cases that mentioned Torrey to learn whether they had spoken of it approvingly or disapprovingly on this point. In fact his research disclosed a series of subsequent cases in Vermont that supported Torrey's basic position. Mr. Lisman was now satisfied that the driving while under suspension conviction was not the obstacle he had feared.

The Torrey episode provides a basic idea of the way in which research for precedent is carried out, although these tasks are rarely performed so mechanically and the results are rarely so clear cut as in our example. Following similar techniques, Mr. Lisman found some support for these other legal positions: the charges reported in the newspaper, if not true, would be serious enough to warrant legal relief; the newspaper's inadvertence in making the error would not destroy the case; and the newspaper and the employee who made the error are both responsible for it. Mr. Lisman was now in possession of enough facts (from his investigations) and law (from his research) to be able to present a persuasive case against both the employee (who turns out to be the reporter) and the newspaper. It is unlikely, however, that an individual reporter would be solvent enough to be worth suing, and Mr. Lisman decided to direct his attack solely against the owner of the newspaper, a corporation named the "St. Albans Publishing Co., Inc."

The sequence of steps in these last two sections has not been random; it reflects the hierarchy of governmental power. Specifically, one must look to federal law first because the states hold a residual position in this relationship. And whether the particular case happens to fit within the federal or the state's province, the research done *within* that sovereign's law must follow the path set out. In other words, the first recourse within any sovereign legal system is to its constitution. If the constitution fails to answer our question, we look to the enactments of the legislature, our elected body of rule makers. If they have spoken on a matter, the courts must follow the legislative directive. Similarly, if the legislature has set up administrative agencies which in turn have promulgated regulations, then the courts must follow these regulations. It is only when no other body with valid law-making powers has acted within an area that the courts themselves may undertake a direct law-making function—as in this case.

E. CHOOSING A COURT SYSTEM

Now that Mr. Lisman has decided against whom he will press Sgt. Towle's claim, how should he proceed? He could file suit immediately but that takes some effort and costs money and might turn out to be unnecessary. Perhaps he can convince the newspaper owner of his liability and reach an agreement out of court on an appropriate amount of damages. Recent studies suggest that some two-thirds of all disputes are settled without any formal legal action. The overwhelming majority of these are settled by informal bargaining and compromise between the parties or their attorneys. Furthermore, when settlement is not forthcoming at this stage, the filing of suit may hasten serious settlement discussions. Initial negotiations were unavailing in the Towle case, so Mr. Lisman decided to bring suit. Although we know that Vermont law applies, we now have another *and distinct* problem. Mr. Lisman must decide in which court he can sue—if he has any choice. Again, the first question is whether the suit is to be brought in a state court or in a federal court. We have a nationwide network of 93 federal trial courts called "district courts." Each state also has its own corresponding trial court structure. As we shall see, there are also higher federal and state courts to which judgments of the trial courts may be appealed.

It is not essential that a federal system have two overlapping judiciaries. Other federal systems, those of Canada, India, and Switzerland for example, have local trial courts and appellate courts with a single national supreme court at the top. In these countries, all cases must be brought in local courts and those having federal implications may ultimately go to the national supreme court. Indeed, the framers of the Constitution of the United States left this matter to Congress. Article III, Section 1 provides that

> The judicial power of the United States shall be vested in one Supreme Court, and in such inferior courts as the Congress may from time to time ordain and establish.

Thus the only federal court whose existence is required by the Constitution is the Supreme Court of the United States. This Court was essential to resolve disputes between states, to provide uniformity on national matters, and to give effect to the supremacy clause of Article VI, Section 2, quoted earlier.

The federal courts that do exist are not available to all litigants or for all cases. Article III, Section 2 limits the federal judicial power:

> The judicial power shall extend to all cases in law and equity arising under this Constitution, the laws of the United States, and treaties made, or which shall be made, under their authority; to all cases affecting ambassadors, other public ministers and consuls; to all cases of admiralty and maritime jurisdiction; to controversies to which the United States shall be a party; to controversies between two or more States; between a State and citizens of another State; between citizens of different States; between citizens of the same State claiming lands under grants of different States; and between a State, or the citizens thereof, and foreign states, citizens, or subjects.

In a unitary state there is no doubt about the scope of judicial power; it will be co-extensive with the legislative power of the state. Indeed in Federalist No. 80, Alexander Hamilton says that "if there are such things as political axioms, the propriety of the judicial power of a government being co-extensive with its legislative, may be ranked among the number." There is no logic to empowering the legislature of a state to regulate contract law unless the judicial power of that state encompasses the power to enforce these laws and adjudicate disputes arising out of them.

With this axiom in mind, reread the Constitutional provision just quoted. So far as federal judicial power is granted for federal questions arising under the federal Constitution or federal statutes, the axiom holds. Other judicial grants, however, exceed federal legislative power. By far the most important exception to the axiom is the extension of federal adjudicative power to disputes "between citizens of different States."

The framers of the Constitution might well have been skeptical about the fairness with which state courts would adjudicate disputes between their citizens and those of other states. Certainly the public was concerned and there was fear that merchants would not engage in commerce in other states without being assured of recourse to the federal judicial power should a dispute arise. Today, however, the incursion on the state's power effected by federal jurisdiction in "diversity of citizenship" cases is not so great as might initially appear, because a federal court deciding a "diversity" case *must* try to decide the case as it anticipates it would be decided by the state court in the state in which the federal court is located. This means that if a diversity case is brought in the federal court located in Vermont, the federal court must attempt to decide the case as it thinks the state courts of Vermont would decide it. Thus, the person invoking the federal court's jurisdiction because of diverse citizenship should not expect to have a different set of legal rules used to decide his case; he should expect only that the federal court will offer him a neutral forum.

Concerns about local bias might justify making such disputes federal cases, but does this require a separate array of federal courts? Why could not the states in the first instance adjudicate disputes involving outsiders, with appeals to the Supreme Court of the United States permitted in cases in which there was a claim of bias? One of the first acts of the First Congress, however, was to create a national network of federal trial courts (now called District Courts), establishing a federal presence in the form of a Court House to go with the Post Office and other manifestations of the new national government. In addition to symbolism it was efficient to increase the likelihood of a fair trial at the outset and thus reduce the incidence of appeals. Moreover, the division of function between trial and appellate courts makes it hard for the latter to discern in the record the more subtle manifestations of bias or unfairness in the courtroom.

Although the federal court in Vermont is situated within the state boundaries, and the federal judge is a member of the Vermont Bar, and jurors are Vermont residents, several circumstances might still make the federal court a fairer forum than the state court. Federal judges have life tenure, whereas many state judges—some elected, some appointed—serve limited terms and are dependent upon popular favor for their continuation in office. Federal courts are located in urban areas, yielding a more broadly-based panel of jurors and a less provincial atmosphere. It is also important to consider the litigant's perception of justice. A litigant rarely blames his defeat on the weakness of his case. For a litigant who fails in the state courts of another state, one of the readiest available excuses is the prejudice of that state. Such interstate hostility would have undermined early Congressional efforts to forge a sense of national unity.

Despite recent suggestions that the need for diversity of citizenship jurisdiction has waned, Congress has been unwilling to eliminate it. It has, however, taken several steps to eliminate diversity jurisdiction in cases involving only small sums and in others in which the likelihood of interstate bias was remote.

Before the Civil War, diversity jurisdiction was the only significant function of the federal courts. After the war, the central government's growing dominance was reflected in the grant to federal courts of jurisdiction to adjudicate cases involving federal substantive law—matters over which Congress has the power to legislate. In most cases the plaintiff may decide whether to sue in state or in federal court. One example is the group of cases involving interstate commerce—one of Congress' broadest legislative powers.

A second, and quite limited, group of cases may be brought only in federal courts. State courts have been denied jurisdiction to hear cases in this category. For example, the Constitution empowered Congress to pass patent and copyright legislation—a power that Congress exercised. Not content with making substantive rules about who may obtain copyrights and how, Congress also provided that all cases involving copyright disputes *must* be brought in the *federal* court system. It is important to recognize that the question of who shall make copyright law is entirely separate from the question of which court should hear copyright disputes; Congress *could* have provided that all copyright disputes must be brought in *state* courts—a clear violation of Hamilton's axiom. The requirement that these cases be brought in federal court may be attributable to the importance of national uniformity in the resolution of such disputes. It might also have been hoped that wiser decisions would result from having a relatively select group of judges deciding such difficult cases. In particularly complex areas, such as taxation and customs, specialized federal courts have been created.

There is a residual third group of cases in which federal courts have jurisdiction only if some unspecified federal law is involved and the amount in dispute exceeds $10,000. The implication is that these areas would be important enough to warrant federal court adjudication only when a relatively large amount is involved.

The crucial point is that just because Congress has legislated in a particular area, it does not follow that all disputes arising from that legislation must be, or even may be, resolved in federal court. That is a distinct and often complex question because of the nature of our federal system.

Since Sgt. Towle was a Vermont resident and the St. Albans Publishing Co. was a Vermont corporation, and its editors and reporters were all presumably Vermont residents, federal jurisdiction based on diversity of citizenship would not be possible. Nor does this case come within the other group since no federal law question is presented. Thus, Mr. Lisman in the Towle case had no choice and had to sue in a state court of Vermont.

F. CHOOSING THE CORRECT COURT

Even after concluding that suit must be brought in some Vermont court, there is still the question of which court. Mr. Lisman was confronted with three types of trial court: justice of the peace court, municipal court, and county court. The justice court's jurisdiction was provided in 4 V.S. § 503:

> A justice [of the peace] shall have jurisdiction of actions of a civil nature where the debt or other matter in demand does not exceed $200.00, except actions for slanderous words, false imprisonment, replevin for goods and chattels when the value thereof exceeds the sum of $20.00, and where the title to land is concerned, and shall have jurisdiction of actions for trespass on the freehold where the sum in demand does not exceed $20.00.

Mr. Lisman would quickly observe that his case was excluded from the court's jurisdiction because he had tentatively estimated the damages in the thousands of dollars.

The jurisdiction of the municipal court was provided in 4 V.S. § 422:

> A municipal court shall have jurisdiction of actions at law of a civil nature wherein the debt or demand is not over $500.00 and wherein the title to real estate is not involved, if either of the parties thereto, at the time such action is commenced, resides within the territorial jurisdiction of such court or if all parties reside without the state.

Again Mr. Lisman would quickly recognize that the municipal court was not the proper court.

Since all the requirements of its jurisdictional statute, 4 V.S. § 113, are met, the county court is the proper place for suit:

> Each county court within the several counties shall have original and exclusive jurisdiction of all original civil actions, except those made cognizable by a justice or municipal court. . . .

Franklin '68 Pamph. FP—3

Of course, as implied in the statute, we have still another question: which county court? Every state has legislation regulating this subject, which is known as "venue" (pronounced as in "menu"). The plaintiff can gain a tactical advantage by picking a place inconvenient to the defendant and his witnesses—especially in a large state. To limit this the larger states have complex venue rules. Would the following Vermont statute be adequate in California? In Vermont, 12 V.S. § 402 provides:

> An action before the county court shall be brought in the county in which one of the parties resides, if either resides in the state; otherwise, on motion, the writ shall abate. If neither party resides in the state, the action may be brought in any county.   .   .   .

The phrase "on motion the writ shall abate" means that if venue is placed in the wrong court, the court will "abate" or dismiss the suit only if the other party objects. If, however, the case is brought at the wrong level of court, even though neither lawyer objects, the judge will dismiss the case or, perhaps, transfer it to the correct court if he realizes the mistake. Why should the judge act on his own when jurisdiction is improper, but wait for an objection when the venue is improper?

The statute gives Mr. Lisman a choice because by the time of suit Sgt. Towle had moved to the town of Milton in Chittenden County. The defendant corporation was a resident of the city of St. Albans in Franklin County. Thus under the "venue" provision Mr. Lisman could sue either in the Chittenden County court in Burlington or 28 miles away in the Franklin County court in St. Albans. What factors might be relevant in deciding between them?

G.   COMMENCING THE ACTION

In fact Mr. Lisman decided to sue in the Chittenden County court. How does he implement that decision? The plaintiff's attorney must do two things: (1) commence the "pleading" stage by putting in writing the plaintiff's "complaint" and what he wants from the defendant; and (2) take steps to bring this "complaint" to the defendant's attention. Statutes prescribe detailed procedures to maximize the likelihood that the defendant will learn that he is being sued. The court satisfies itself that the document has been properly "served" by a document known as a "return." The interplay of these functions may be seen in the document that follows, which combines the admonition to "serve" the papers, the thrust of plaintiff's "complaint," and finally an order to the defendant. (One warning—although the first line of the document talks about seizing the goods of the defendant and then letting the defendant know, the documents in this case were served without seizing any property. Attorneys often use printed forms with blanks filled in at crucial points. The standard Vermont forms for commencing this type of suit call for seizing property—a practice most commonly invoked when the plaintiff fears that the defendant might otherwise spirit all his assets away and be unable to satisfy any judgment plaintiff obtains. Since the defendant here was a reputable and successful business, there was no need to seize property.)

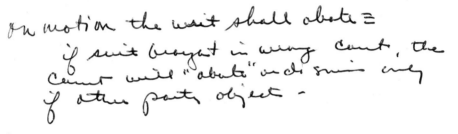

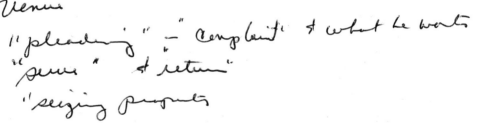

STATE OF VERMONT

CHITTENDEN COUNTY

To any Sheriff or Constable in the State, or to an indifferent person.

GREETING:

By the Authority of the State of Vermont, You are hereby commanded to attach the goods, chattels or estate of   ST. ALBANS   PUBLISHING CO., INC., a corporation organized and existing   under the laws of the State of Vermont, with principal office in   City of St. Albans,   in the County of _Franklin_ in the State of Vermont to the value of   fifteen thousand   dollars and _them_ notify thereof according to law; and also notify _them_ to appear before the _Chittenden_ County Court at _Burlington_ within and for the County of _Chittenden_ and also to notify _them_ to cause _their_ appearance herein, to be entered with the clerk of said Court, on or before the expiration of forty-two days from the date hereof, then and there in said Court to answer to

RONALD W. TOWLE, of Milton, in the County of Chittenden

In an action of tort, for that at St. Albans, on the 25th day of November, 1957, the defendant falsely published the following story: "Ronald Towle, of Fairfax, an air policeman, formerly of Enosburg, pleaded guilty to driving while intoxicated. He paid a fine of $50 and costs of $12.30." The said publication was false and was also made of and concerning the plaintiff. In truth and fact, the plaintiff did not plead guilty to driving while intoxicated in any court or elsewhere.

Thereafter, on the 26th day of November, 1957, without withdrawing or correcting its former publication, the defendant published the following story: "A man who five months ago was suspended from the Franklin County Sheriffs' Patrol was arraigned in Municipal Court here yesterday; pleading guilty to driving for the past nine years on a suspended license . . . Ronald Towle, of Fairfax, who was dropped from the Patrol in June for "misuse of authority" was brought before Municipal Court Judge Carl S. Gregg and was fined $50, plus costs."

The said publication further stated: "Finn [the sheriff of Franklin County] said this morning his [meaning the plaintiff] permit from the Department of Public Safety was withdrawn when he was dropped from the Patrol for the misuse of authority and on order of the office of Strategic Information USAF. Ft. Ethan Allen, Vt."

Statements in the aforesaid publication that the plaintiff was dropped from the Franklin County Sheriffs' Patrol for misuse of authority were false. In truth and fact, the plaintiff was not dropped from said Patrol for misuse of authority.

By reason of the aforesaid false publications, the plaintiff has been held up to ridicule, contempt and hatred; became physically ill; was forced to close his business as a radio and television repair man; lost his credit; and has been greatly disturbed in mind.

To the damage of the plaintiff, as he says, fifteen thousand dollars, for the recovery of which, with just costs, the plaintiff brings this suit.

Fail not, but service and return make within twenty-one days from the date hereof.

Dated at Burlington in the County of Chittenden the 15th day of August 19 58.

(signed) Robert J. Rousseau
Clerk

First look at the substantive part of the document (or writ). The complaint serves several functions. One is to show the Chittenden County court that it has "jurisdiction" over the case (the demand is for $15,000) and that "venue" is proper (Sgt. Towle now lives in Milton). A second function of the complaint is to limit the scope of the controversy and to give notice of plaintiff's claim. This is how the defendant learns what contentions he must meet. Notice that the complaint cites no cases or statutes but only relates what the plaintiff contends are the relevant *facts*. This form of pleading conforms to Vermont's statutory requirement, 12 V.S. § 1021, that the complaint "set forth in brief and simple language the facts relied upon and the relief demanded."

You may be wondering how Mr. Lisman arrived at the damage figure of $15,000. Usually the figure is substantially more than the case's realistic value in order to encourage settlement. Beyond this psychological ploy, the attorney must be certain that the figure is at least adequate to cover the plaintiff's losses. In a defamation case this is hard to assess because there are few tangible items such as the medical bills or lost wages that accompany personal injury cases, or loss of a specific profit in breach of contract cases. Yet there are elements of specific loss in the Towle case, as we shall see, plus likely, but not precisely measurable, reputational harm. Finally, there is an attorney's fee to be considered. In the United States each party usually pays his own attorney fees, and since Mr. Lisman had agreed to represent his client on a contingent basis, his fee must come from the suit's proceeds. In many countries, including England, the losing party in a litigation must pay reasonable attorney's fees incurred by the winning party. What are the advantages and disadvantages of this rule as against the general American rule that each party bears his own legal costs?

Another reason for a figure on the high side is that in some states a plaintiff may not recover from the defendant any amount greater than he demanded in the complaint. Even though courts are often generous in allowing parties to "amend" their pleadings in the light of newly found facts, it is safest to ask for "enough" at the outset.

Let's turn now to the procedural part of the pleading. One of the most deeply held notions of our Anglo-American jurisprudential heritage is that in order for a court to adjudicate a claim against an individual or a corporation (and we treat corporations as persons for this purpose) the court must obtain "jurisdiction" over the body of the defendant. Historically this was done in a physical way: the defendant was brought before the court which then had "jurisdiction" (power) to adjudicate the case. We no longer require such physical presence but we do generally require the plaintiff to show that the defendant is within the court's power.

The modern manifestations of this attitude may be seen in the Towle case. In effect, the plaintiff served a "summons" upon the defendant telling him that an action had been started against him and the nature of the action, and ordering him to do something within 42 days from August 15, 1958. Since the plaintiff is given only 21 of those days to serve the papers, this assures the defendant at least 21 days to contemplate his response.

H. MECHANICS OF SERVICE

The rules about how to serve these papers on the defendant are complex. The ideal would be to give the papers to the defendant personally to be sure he acquires actual knowledge of the proceeding against him. But even here there would be exceptions for such extraordinary cases as children, the insane, and defendants who have left the state. For a corporate defendant, as in our case, 12 V.S. § 813 provides that "writs against a corporation . . . shall be served by leaving a copy with the clerk thereof. . . ." By statute, every Vermont corporation is required to have a "clerk."

How does the court find out whether service was in fact properly made within the required 21 day period? The process server, a deputy sheriff, "attested" that within the 21 days, on August 22, 1958, he served a copy of these papers on the defendant corporation by delivering to its clerk, Mr. William J. Clark, a copy of these papers and that he is now returning another set of them to the court.

Notice that with the signature of the clerk of the Chittenden County Court, Robert J. Rousseau, on the complaint the court becomes involved in this case for the first time. In other states the pleadings may be handled entirely by the lawyers and the court might not even know a dispute exists until the parties request a courtroom for the trial.

I. AN IMPORTANT DIGRESSION

The Towle case had no federal aspect because all of the parties
were in Vermont when the action occurred and are still in Vermont. But sometimes the case becomes more complicated. What
should Sgt. Towle have done if he was run down in Vermont by a
vacationing Nebraska automobile driver who immediately returned home? *Must* Sgt. Towle go to the Nebraska state courts—or,
if he is reasonably demanding over $10,000, to the federal courts
in Nebraska? If the case were tried in the Nebraska state courts
or federal court, those courts would use local procedural law for
such things as serving papers and determining venue, but would
have to use Vermont's law of automobile accidents because the
accident occurred there. Of course, Nebraska courts are more
familiar with Nebraska law than with Vermont law but with
some help from the lawyers, the court would learn Vermont law
and decide the case as though it were a Vermont court. Lawyers
call this "choice of law" and the general rule would be that
wherever the suit is brought because of the parties' diverse citizenship, that court would use the law of the place where the disputed act occurred. The subject has other facets that are even
more complicated, but this example gives you a general idea of
the distinction between the matter of which court to go to in
order to get "jurisdiction" over the defendant, and which state's
law that court will use to decide the rights of the parties.

So far, this discussion has been premised on the assumption
that Sgt. Towle was willing to sue in Nebraska. That is especially unlikely when we realize that witnesses to the accident are
probably in Vermont, the police reports are in Vermont, and he is
in Vermont. It will be expensive to sue in Nebraska, and Sgt.
Towle will prefer to bring the case in Vermont. But can he?
If the Nebraska driver should ever return to Vermont then the
plaintiff could gain Vermont jurisdiction over him by serving
him with papers as was done in the actual Towle case. But what
if the Nebraska defendant decides to remain out of Vermont for
the rest of his life? For many years, the plaintiff's only recourse
was to sue in Nebraska. Any action brought and pursued in Vermont without serving the Nebraska defendant in Vermont was a
nullity that the Nebraskan could safely disregard.

Since the 1920's, however, the law has begun to respond to the
increasing mobility of American society and the apparent unfairness of requiring Sgt. Towle to go to Nebraska. Statutes called
"non-resident motorist" statutes now enable the victim to sue in
the state in which the accident occurred. Vermont's version, 12
V.S. §§ 891 and 892, provides:

> § 891. The acceptance by a person of the rights and
> privileges conferred upon him by Titles 19 [Highways]

and 23 [Motor Vehicles], as evidenced by his operating, or causing to be operated, a motor vehicle in this state, shall be deemed equivalent to an appointment by such person of the commissioner of motor vehicles, or his successor in office, to be his true and lawful attorney upon whom may be served all lawful processes in any action or proceeding against such person growing out of any accident or collision in which such person may be involved while operating or causing to be operated a motor vehicle in this state. Such acceptance shall be deemed to be the agreement of such person that any process against him which is so served upon the commissioner shall be of the same legal force and validity as if served on the person personally.

§ 892. Such service of process shall be made by leaving a copy of the process with a fee of $2.00 with the commissioner, or in his office. Such service shall be sufficient service upon the person, provided that a copy of such process with the officer's return thereon, showing service thereof upon the commissioner as provided in this section, is sent by the plaintiff to the defendant by registered mail, and provided further that the plaintiff's affidavit of compliance herewith is filed with the process in court. The commissioner shall file copies served upon him. . . and show upon each copy the day and hour of service thereof.

Although this creates a serious burden on the Nebraska defendant, such statutes have been upheld by the United States Supreme Court as being within the powers of the state in which the alleged wrong took place. The Nebraska courts are then obligated to enforce the judgment, if any, imposed by the Vermont court against the Nebraska defendant. This is required by Article IV, Section 1, of the United States Constitution, which requires that "Full Faith and Credit shall be given in each State to the public Acts, Records, and judicial Proceedings of every other State." Nebraska must accept the Vermont judgment as conclusive once the Vermont resident shows he followed the proper statutory rules in serving his papers. Without such a statute, Nebraska courts need not honor Vermont judgments because "Full Faith and Credit" does not extend to cases in which jurisdiction was not properly obtained over the defendant. Once, however, this statutory procedure has been adopted and followed, the threat of the full faith and credit clause forces the defendant to take some action. Rather than returning to Vermont himself, the defendant who receives the required notice of the Vermont action will probably consult an attorney in Nebraska who will do some preliminary research on the validity of the procedure and then turn the matter over to a Vermont attorney to handle directly. The case will then proceed essentially as though the defendant lived in Vermont.

In which court system must the Nebraska defendant defend his case? Initially, the papers will probably direct him to answer in the state courts of Vermont, but this might raise the same grounds of prejudice against outsiders that we discussed earlier in diversity of citizenship cases. Therefore, just as we permitted a plaintiff suing in another state the privilege of suing in federal court in that other state, we will permit this Nebraska defendant to "remove" his case from the Vermont state court to the Vermont federal court—if it meets the $10,000 minimum.

The motorist statute has been extended to non-resident ventures that either transact or otherwise affect business within the state. Recently, for example, William F. Buckley, a resident of Connecticut, decided to sue the New York Post for libel. Buckley clearly could have gone to New York to file his suit. Instead, he brought suit in Connecticut claiming that the New York Post, though a New York corporation, had considerable circulation and several advertisers in Connecticut. In other words, he claimed that the Post had enough "contacts" with the state of Connecticut so that it was not unfair to the Post to have to defend a libel suit in Connecticut. The court agreed with Buckley and allowed him to sue in Connecticut.

The reasoning behind Mr. Buckley's choice became clear in a statement his attorney made after being given permission to sue in Connecticut. He was afraid that if the case were tried in New York, the jurors would identify with the Post. "We wanted to be in our own ball park . . . in a case where a Connecticut citizen will be judged by a Connecticut jury".

J. THE DEFENDANT'S TURN

When Mr. Clark was served with court papers the defendant officially learned it was being sued. It is possible, though unlikely, that the corporate officers considered at great length what to do. It is much more likely that at the first inkling of trouble the corporation consulted its lawyer, who would then represent it in settlement talks. A publishing company in a substantial business venture probably has an attorney on a continuing, or retainer, basis under which he does general legal work for the corporation. In this case the papers were turned over to John Mulvey, an attorney who practiced by himself in St. Albans. Mr. Mulvey was born in 1916, attended Fordham University in New York City and received his law degree from Boston College. He was admitted to the Vermont bar in 1948. (Shortly after the Towle case was concluded Mr. Mulvey was elected Probate Judge of Franklin County.)

Mr. Mulvey's first action was probably to interview the reporters and other witnesses to assess the basic elements of Sgt. Towle's complaint. At this point he *might* have decided that the newspaper had indeed libeled Sgt. Towle, had no adequate legal defenses, and that the $15,000 sought was entirely reasonable in view of the harm suffered. If Mr. Mulvey had reached these conclusions he would have advised his client that the case was hopeless and that defense costs would be substantial and the outlook for success minimal. If the client agreed, Mr. Mulvey might have called Mr. Lisman to settle the case or might have suffered a "default judgment" by taking no action before the 42-day deadline of September 26, 1958.

In the latter instance the plaintiff, after 42 days, would have "moved" for a judicial ruling that he was entitled to $15,000 because of the defendant's failure to appear. After a lawsuit has been started, a party who believes that he is entitled to some judicial action brings this contention to the court's attention by a "motion". The reasons are set forth in writing with the demanded remedy. Thus, if the defendant had failed to do anything within 42 days, the plaintiff would "file a motion" setting forth the facts of the default and demanding that he be awarded judgment. The plaintiff would be called the "moving party" or the "movant." The "motion" is a very important procedure and we shall see it used frequently.

The court, once assured that the defendant had indeed learned of the suit (by the "return of process"), could assume that he had no adequate response and would award the plaintiff $15,000. Notice again that this would not have happened automatically; the plaintiff would have to press his claim and provide some proof that the $15,000 fairly measured the plaintiff's loss. (If a defendant defaults because of forgetfulness, the court may permit him to reopen the case and start again if he has an arguable defense to make).

K. CHOOSING A DEFENSE

Almost always, though, the defendant asserts that there are mistakes or inaccuracies in the plaintiff's case in one *or more* of four categories: (1) technical objections unrelated to the merits of the case; (2) disputes about the underlying legal rules implicit in the plaintiff's complaint; (3) claims that the plaintiff's fact allegations are not true or that he has omitted some vital facts; and (4) claims that the damages sought are too high. We shall look at how the defendant raises each contention.

(1). The first of these, technical objections, includes assertions that service was on the wrong party, or by mail when it had to be in person, or that venue is incorrectly placed. Each might be the subject of a motion to dismiss the case. Most of these claims would be only delaying tactics because the plaintiff could cure the defect and start again. One technical defense, however, the assertion that the statute of limitations has run, would be fatal to the plaintiff's case. He cannot start again; it is already too late.

(2). Defendant raises his objections to the underlying legal theory of the complaint by a challenge in which he is willing to assume that all of the *facts* alleged in the plaintiff's complaint are true, but argues that they don't show that the defendant has done anything for which the law will hold him accountable. This motion, called a "demurrer" or "a motion to dismiss for failure to state a claim on which relief can be granted," essentially says "so what?"

This important device cuts quickly to the heart of the case and is the most common way courts decide legal questions. Although Sgt. Towle's complaint states no legal rules we may be sure that Mr. Lisman studied the relevant rules carefully to find out what facts he had to put in the complaint. He did not include the color of Sgt. Towle's eyes or his height because he found nothing in his research to indicate these were legally relevant. When Mr. Mulvey gets a copy of the complaint he, too, will search the relevant legal authorities to see if Mr. Lisman omitted some essential element. If he believes he has found one he will "demur," i. e., he will assert that "even if plaintiff is correct in all the facts he states, he has not given the court any reason to do anything to my client." For example, if Mr. Mulvey thought that his legal research had uncovered a proposition that defendants need pay only for intentional defamations, then he might demur, or make a motion to dismiss, in which he asserted that the complaint had a fatal flaw in that it made no charge of deliberate defamation. Mr. Lisman would file papers arguing that Mr. Mulvey was wrong and that deliberate action was not essential.

The judge would then decide the question, always acting on the assumption that all of the facts in the complaint are true. If he agreed with Mr. Mulvey the judge would dismiss the case and avoid the substantial time and effort consumed in a trial. Since the trial's function is to resolve disputed facts, there is no need for a trial when the plaintiff will lose even if his alleged facts are all true.

The plaintiff is unlikely to allege facts in his complaint that he has no hope of proving at the trial; his loss at trial will make his avoidance of the defendant's demurrer a Pyrrhic victory. Moreover, 12 V.S. § 1022 provides that "Allegations or denials, made without reasonable cause and found untrue, shall subject the party pleading the same to reasonable costs, to be taxed as directed by the court." On the other hand, unprovable allegations are sometimes made in the hope that fear of suit will induce some settlement offer from the defendant.

(3). In the third possible situation, that in which defendant disputes the accuracy or completeness of the alleged *facts*, defendant files an "answer" that may take several different forms. He may make a "general denial" of the "material" allegations in the plaintiff's complaint, admitting such things as the plaintiff's name and address but denying the truth of any allegations essential to recovery. Or the defendant may "answer" by specific denials that identify allegations he claims to be untrue, implicitly admitting the others. If the plaintiff's allegations look sufficient on paper, but the defendant thinks that the plaintiff has omitted crucial facts, defendant may complete the story by alleging these new facts as an "affirmative defense." For example, in an automobile accident the plaintiff's complaint may allege that the defendant was speeding and yet say nothing about his own conduct. In addition to denying that he was speeding, defendant could allege as an affirmative defense that plaintiff had tried to commit suicide by throwing himself in the path of defendant's car.

(4). The fourth concern of the defendant, that the damages alleged are too high, is a variant of the third category. Plaintiff's fact allegation of how seriously he has been damaged may be controverted in the way suggested above by an "answer." The difference is that an "answer" in the third situation, if accurate, would completely bar the plaintiff from recovery. If, however, defendant's contention is only that the damages claimed are too high, then defendant can only hope to avoid paying all that plaintiff claims, but he admits he must pay *something*.

Of course, as suggested earlier, often the defendant will try more than one of these four approaches—and sometimes all of them. For example, first he may make a motion that the venue is wrongly placed. If that fails, he may file an "answer" denying some fact allegations in plaintiff's complaint and alleging some new facts relating either to the merits or the damages, or both.

Within the 42-day period Mr. Mulvey filed a document in court stating that he had been retained to represent the defendant. Apparently he then negotiated with Mr. Lisman for more time to investigate and prepare his defense. Perhaps Mr. Mulvey was especially busy and could not turn immediately to this case, or perhaps some important parties were out of town. In any event, Mr. Lisman did not insist upon the 42-day limit and the court took no action because Mr. Lisman sought none.

Finally, on April 7, 1959, the defendant filed the following pleading:

STATE OF VERMONT

CHITTENDEN COUNTY

RONALD W. TOWLE

v.

ST. ALBANS PUBLISHING COMPANY, INC.

CHITTENDEN COUNTY COURT

DOCKET NO. 7348

ANSWER

1. Now comes the Defendant, by its Attorney, and denies each and every material allegation set forth in the Plaintiff's Complaint.

2. Now comes the Defendant as aforesaid and for a further defense alleges that the matter published by the Defendant was true except that it, through inadvertence, stated that the Plaintiff had, on November 25, 1957, pleaded guilty to and had been convicted of "Driving While Intoxicated", while, in fact, the said Plaintiff had on that date and at the Franklin Municipal Court pleaded guilty to the crime of "Driving While Under Suspension", to wit, that he, at Fairfax, "did then and there operate a motor vehicle on and over a public highway, to wit, the main road leading from Fairfax to Westford, while his right to operate a motor vehicle had been suspended or revoked by the Commissioner of Motor Vehicles for the State of Vermont", and the Plaintiff was sentenced to pay a fine of Fifty Dollars plus costs.

3. The article appearing in the Defendant's newspaper on November 26, 1957, was believed by the Defendant to be true as published and the Defendant alleges that it is true and is a fair comment upon a public hearing, to wit, the hearing held by the Franklin Municipal Court on November 25, 1957, wherein the Plaintiff had pleaded guilty to the crime of operating a motor vehicle while his license was suspended as set forth in paragraph 2.

4. The Defendant denies that the plaintiff was damaged in the manner and form as set forth in the Complaint and puts itself upon the country.

Dated at St. Albans, this 4th day of April, 1959.

ST. ALBANS PUBLISHING COMPANY, INC.

/s/ John Mulvey

By _____

Its Attorney

Why did Mr. Mulvey file an answer instead of some other defense? In his answer he first denied generally every material allegation. This alone, however, would be insufficient to raise the defense of truth because the rule in Vermont is that truth is an affirmative defense that must be pleaded and proven by the defendant. Thus, in Paragraph 2, the defendant pleaded that all of the first story was true except that through inadvertence the story reported the wrong charge. In Paragraph 3 the defendant alleged that the second story was believed true and is still believed to be true by the defendant. Finally, the defendant denied the extent of damages.

The issues that separate the parties are now becoming clear. As to the second story there is a dispute about the relations between Sgt. Towle and the sheriff's patrol. The plaintiff asserts that he was not "dropped from the patrol for misuse of authority" and the defendant claims that he was. If the defendant can establish the truth of this charge it will not be liable for the second article and will win that part of the case. There is still some ambiguity that continues through the case concerning the first story. Defendant does not deny the error in the first story, but introduces a new argument: that the error occurred "through inadvertence." Is the defendant implying that inadvertence would relieve it from all liability? Or that the two crimes are equally serious so that no harm was done? If so, we shall see that these are both incorrect rules of law. Or is defendant pleading "inadvertence" to support the argument that even though defendant is liable for the first story, the damages should be low because the harm was not deliberate? If the latter interpretation is correct, then the defendant has in effect admitted that it is liable for *some* amount of money as a result of the first story.

It is fair to say that after defendant's answer was filed the disputes had been narrowed to two: the extent of damages suffered by the plaintiff as a result of the first story, and whether the second story was true. If the second story was not true then damages would also have to be assessed for that story. (If further narrowing of issues had been possible, plaintiff might have filed another pleading called a "reply.") Our next question is how these remaining disputes are to be resolved.

L. PRE-TRIAL ACTIVITIES

After the written pleadings have been completed what happens next? At this point one or more of several "pre-trial" procedures may be followed.

(1) *Judgment on the Pleadings.*—Either party may make a "motion for judgment on the pleadings." This has many of the aspects of the demurrer that we talked about earlier. The party making the motion asserts that with all the pleadings filed, no fact disputes remain so that there is no reason for a trial and the judge should decide the case now. No such motion was made by either party in the Towle case. Why?

(2) *Discovery.*—If the case cannot be disposed of on the pleadings, this means that fact disputes remain and the case must proceed to trial to resolve these disputes. Unfortunately, most of the layman's ideas about a trial are derived from criminal trials dramatized on television or in fiction. The spectacle of the surprise witness racing into court at the last minute to save the day is rare.

In *civil* cases in the last 30 years there has been a notable movement away from the "sporting" theory of litigation and toward a more rational approach to settling disputes. (Although there has been some attention to discovery in the criminal area, it has been less extensive than in the civil area and is likely to remain so. Why?) Several specific devices are included under the generic name "discovery." By submitting written questions, called "interrogatories," to those who may know something about the case, the parties may learn the names of others who may have useful information about the case. A second device is the "deposition" by which the attorneys orally question prospective witnesses. A transcript of the deposition may be used at trial if the witness is not available; it might also be used to impugn the credibility of a witness who does appear but gives a different story on the witness stand. Third, the parties may be required to produce documents or other physical evidence that may be relevant. Moreover, when one party's physical condition is an issue, he may be forced to undergo examination by the other party's physician. If these procedures lead a litigant to believe that some of his adversary's denials of fact are frivolous, he may request the adversary to admit them. If the adversary unreasonably refuses, he may have to pay any expenses the requesting party incurs in proving these facts.

The goals of these discovery procedures include eliminating the surprise element from litigation by requiring disclosure of all relevant evidence before trial; narrowing the scope of the controversy still further by gaining admissions so that the trial itself can be more sharply focused; preserving testimony and evidence against loss, destruction or unavailability; and enhancing prospects for a settlement without trial by requiring each party to show his cards to the other. These procedures are used widely in civil cases, but were not used in Towle. Why not?

(3) *Summary Judgment.*—The "motion for summary judgment" is a common way to end a case without a full-dress courtroom trial. This motion tells the court that the party making it admits that there is an *apparent* dispute of fact in the pleadings, but he contends that the fact dispute is illusory. In order to establish this point the moving party will present to the court information obtained during the "discovery" procedure and any additional sworn statements (affidavits) and documents that support the contention that there is no genuine issue of fact worthy of a trial. The opponent has an opportunity to respond by counter affidavits but he must usually do more than call the other side's statements "lies;" he must set forth specific facts showing the existence of a genuine issue for trial. What types of disputes will summary judgment procedure handle best?

It was suggested earlier that parties had little to gain by pleading the existence of facts they could not hope to prove at trial. Yet there may be some hidden gains. From the defendant's side, denying allegations he thinks true may result in delaying the "day of judgment." During this delay defendant can use the money that is in dispute—often without paying interest. From the plaintiff's side, even a groundless suit costs money to defend. Thus, the suit may acquire a nuisance value that will induce the defendant to offer a token settlement to be rid of the case. The "motion for summary judgment" provides a quick, easy method of showing that no genuine issue remains to warrant a trial—and thus thwarts these devious practices. No motion for summary judgment was made in the Towle case. Why not?

(4) *Pre-Trial Conferences.*—Sgt. Towle's case is now well on its way to the courtroom. In an effort to narrow the issues still further there may be a "pre-trial conference" before the case is to be tried. The attorneys and the judge meet informally in the judge's chambers. The judge will attempt to identify the remaining issues and speed the trial by having documentary evidence examined and identified before trial. There is often, however, another purpose of this conference: exploration of out-of-court settlement. To facilitate settlements, the law generally declares all evidence of abortive settlement negotiations inadmissible at trial. Some judges believe they should play little or no part in settlement talks and leave this to the lawyers. Other judges view encouragement of settlements as one of their functions and may put considerable pressure on the attorneys to reach a settlement by bringing the settlement figures closer to-

gether and emphasizing the respective strengths and weaknesses in each position. Finally, if necessary a convenient date for trial will be set.

On September 9, 1959, the pre-trial conference was held in the case of Towle v. St. Albans Publishing Co. The principal purpose of the conference was to identify certain documents that might be used at the trial. During the conference settlement discussions were held and Mr. Lisman said that he was willing to recommend to his client a settlement for $1,500. Why is this sum so low? Mr. Mulvey, however, indicated that the defendant was not inclined to offer anything at this time.

There is still time for settlement, however, and the vast majority of cases do settle before trial. Although the attorney can only advise his client on the desirability of a particular settlement offer, the attorney's judgment is almost always accepted. The client knows little about what makes a "good settlement" but a good attorney develops this sense. The settlement is largely a function of the likelihood of ultimate success, the potential impact of total defeat for either party, the distastefulness of a lengthy legal struggle, and the expense of continued legal representation. A few hours after the pre-trial conference Mr. Lisman discussed settlement at some length with Sgt. Towle and discovered that the Sergeant was thinking in terms of about $2,000. As a result of this conference, Mr. Lisman on September tenth sent the following letter to Mr. Mulvey.

September 10, 1959

John Mulvey, Esq.,
Attorney at Law
St. Albans, Vt.

Dear John:

Re: Towle vs. St. Albans Publishing Co.

I was able to visit with Sgt. Towle yesterday afternoon. He has authorized me to submit an offer for settlement purposes of $2,000. This offer is made solely for purpose of settlement.

I think it ought to be of interest to your client, as it is less than what his liability would be if the jury gave us the deductible amount or more, which, of course, is a distinct probability in this case. Sgt. Towle has considerable pecuniary loss as a result of the libel which forced him to leave town, caused moving expense and required him to close down his business there and sell his home, on which he took a licking of more than $1,000 on its original cost.

Will you please let me know your client's reaction as soon as possible as Judge Hill tells me that we are likely to be reached before the end of the month.

With kind regards.

Sincerely yours,

/signed/

Louis Lisman

Since Mr. Mulvey had refused an offer of $1,500 on September ninth, it was highly unlikely that his client would be willing to pay $2,000 on September tenth. Indeed, Mr. Mulvey replied to the letter by telephone and stated that his client declined to pay anything.

With regard to settlement the case was unusual in two respects: the plaintiff's demand was going up instead of down and the defendant was refusing to make any offer whatsoever. The plaintiff's conduct may be explained by the fact that Mr. Lisman's first recommendation was apparently made without a prior discussion of specific figures with his client and in their subsequent discussion Sgt. Towle may have been unwilling to reduce his $2,000 claim. Another possible explanation is that the discussions at the pre-trial conference led Mr. Lisman on reflection to believe that his case was somewhat stronger than he had previously thought. Keep in mind that the attorney only advises the client and must honor his requests or cease to represent him. While it is true that the attorney's advice is almost always accepted, he must not act so as to affect his client's interest without prior consent. If an impasse develops in which the client refuses to follow the attorney's advice, the attorney must either accede to the client's wishes or remove himself from the case. If he leaves the case the lawyer must not do so without sufficient notice to the client to permit him to protect himself. How does this compare with the doctor-patient relationship?

Turning now to the defendant, why was no settlement offer forthcoming? This is particularly difficult to understand in light of the fact that the first story was clearly defamatory and was untrue. We can surmise that two factors played a prominent role in the defendant's decision. The defendant may have thought that Sgt. Towle's reputation had not been hurt to the extent he was claiming and that the jury might well return a nominal verdict. Sometimes in defamation cases a jury returns a verdict of six cents or $1.00 to support the assertion that the story was in error and defamatory but that nevertheless the plaintiff suffered no damage (either because nobody believed the story or it wasn't serious or because the plaintiff's reputation was so bad that the erroneous story did not hurt it any further). Another explanation is suggested by Mr. Lisman's mention in the September tenth letter of a "deductible amount," indicating that the defendant corporation had an insurance policy against liability for defamation. These policies resemble automobile liability insurance in that the insurance company agrees to pay for legal liability to others incurred by the insured. A major distinction is that libel insurance usually has a deductible clause and in this case it was $2,500. (This is comparable to conventional automobile collision insurance in which the owner of the car normally pays the first $50 or $100 of his own repair bill.) The effect of the libel policy in this case was that, although Mr. Lisman was asking $15,000 in this complaint, the corporation itself would have to pay only the first $2,500 and insurance would cover the rest. Any incentive for the defendant to settle was thus reduced because any settlement under $2,500 would be paid entirely by the corporation. With only $2,500 at stake perhaps the defendant felt more freedom to hold out for a nominal verdict rather than give up $1,500 or $2,000 without a fight.

Since no pretrial motion terminated the case and since no settlement was forthcoming, the case proceeded to trial on September 24, 1959, before the Honorable William C. Hill, who presided in several county courts. Judge Hill, born in 1917, held the A.B. and LL.B. degrees from New York University. He was admitted to the Vermont bar in 1942 and practiced in Burlington until February 1, 1959, when a joint session of the Vermont Senate and House of Representatives elected him to a two-year term as a Superior Judge. Is this method of selecting judges desirable? How long should the term be?

M. A JURY IS CHOSEN AND THE TRIAL BEGINS

The primary purpose of the trial, as we have seen, is to resolve all remaining fact disputes. Also important, however, is the need to combine these ascertained facts with applicable rules of law. For our purposes there is a clear distinction between questions of fact and questions of law. In an automobile accident, for example, whether or not the defendant went through a red light at the intersection is a question of fact. The consequence of a finding that he did or did not do so is a question of law. In Sgt. Towle's case one fact question is whether the second story was true. The legal question is what happens if the story is found to be true, and what happens if the story is found to be false.

Now we may consider who will decide these questions at the trial. A judge always presides at a trial and decides the applicable questions of law. But fact questions are resolved by a jury, except that if the parties waive jury trial or no jury is permitted in that type of case, the judge will also decide fact questions.

Americans commonly think of the jury as an institution of fundamental importance in the administration of justice. Yet it is fair to suggest that this is because juries are most often used in the two kinds of cases with which laymen have most experience —whether as spectator in a famous criminal case, or as party, witness, or juror in an automobile accident case. You might assume that there are jurors in all criminal cases, but think again. What about traffic offenses? Generally, the right to a jury trial exists only in major criminal cases. On the civil side, the right to a jury trial exists in personal injury cases and is generally exercised. On the other hand, juries are not permitted in divorce cases.

Both the federal and state constitutions guarantee the right to jury trial in some instances. For example, the Sixth Amendment to the federal Constitution guarantees a jury trial in criminal cases while the Seventh Amendment guarantees jury trial in some civil cases. But just because the right is guaranteed does not mean that it must be exercised. In many cases, although the parties have this right they may waive it, preferring to be tried by the judge alone. A party may want a quick trial and the wait for jury trials is almost always longer than that for judge trials. Another consideration might be the greater informality that attends a non-jury trial. After the trial we shall return to a brief consideration of what might have transpired had there been no jury. Vermont's constitution however, recognizes the right to a jury trial in this type of suit "except where parties otherwise agree." That this agreement would not be forthcoming became clear back at the pleading stage when, in the last paragraph of the answer, the defendant said that it "puts itself upon the country." This is a traditional way of indicating defendant's desire for a jury trial. Why do you think the defendant wanted a jury? If you were Mr. Lisman would you want a jury trial?

Since Mr. Mulvey, in fact, asserted his client's right to a jury trial, the first order of business at the trial was to select a jury.

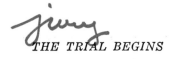

The basic requirement in Vermont is that a prospective juror be in sound physical and mental condition and be an eligible voter. From those who are eligible and do not claim occupational exemption, such as physicians, or are excused for hardship reasons, a panel (or venire) of 25 or 50 persons is directed to appear at the courtroom for the start of the trial. Occasionally an attorney may challenge the entire venire. This is called a "challenge to the array" and occurs when the attorney thinks that the panel has been improperly chosen—as by excluding some eligible group such as Negroes. Although, as we know, certain occupations are overrepresented on juries in proportion to the total population, such as managerial officials and salesmen, and others such as laborers are underrepresented, mere imbalance does not warrant a challenge to the array; systematic exclusion of particular groups must be shown.

If no such challenge is made, 12 veniremen are selected at random. The judge and the attorneys question prospective jurors to determine whether there is reason to disqualify any of them from participating in the case at hand. The judge's role in this process varies, but usually he will tell the panel the bare outline of the case and then ask such formal questions as whether any prospective juror is related to any party or participating attorney. The attorneys may ask whether any prospective juror knows Sgt. Towle or his family, or knows any reporters for the newspaper—or ever worked for the newspaper. They might also ask whether panel members have heard anything about this case from friends so that they might be deeply biased. This questioning, at times called "voir dire," is handled exclusively by the judge in some courts.

When an attorney challenges a specific juror he may use one of two bases. Those we have already talked about are often called "challenges for cause" in which the attorney contends that something has been shown about the specific juror that clearly disqualifies him from participating in the particular case. If the judge agrees with the attorney, the juror is dismissed from sitting on this case. The attorney has an unlimited number of "challenges for cause."

But if the judge refuses to grant the challenge, or if the attorney merely senses a lack of rapport with one of the jurors, he may use a "peremptory challenge" which in effect tells the judge "I can give no reason, but I don't want that particular juror in this case." Peremptory challenges must be exercised carefully because each side usually has only a few. In a criminal trial, for example, the defense attorney might exercise his peremptory challenges against prospective jurors who seem unduly self-righteous or sanctimonious, while the District Attorney might use his to remove persons who strike him as being somewhat non-conformist.

This process continues until 12 eligible jurors have been agreed upon by the attorneys or, in some hotly contested cases, until the lawyers have run out of challenges. In potentially protracted cases, alternate jurors may be chosen to sit so that if a regular juror gets sick the trial may continue uninterrupted. All jurors then take the prescribed oath (12 V.S. § 5803):

> You solemnly swear that you will well and truly try each and every issue which may be given you in charge during the present term of this court, agreeably to the evidence given you in court, and the laws of this state, and true verdicts give; your own counsel and that of your fellows you will duly observe and keep; you will say nothing to any person about the business and matters you may at any time have in charge, but to your fellow jurors, nor will you suffer any one to speak to you about the same but in court; and when you have agreed on a verdict, you will keep it secret until you deliver it in court. So help you God.

Once the jury has been chosen and sworn, we are ready to begin to resolve the remaining fact disputes. The sequence of proving facts at trial generally parallels the pattern of pre-trial pleadings described above. We saw then that the plaintiff had the burden of starting the pleadings, but that the defendant had the burden of pleading the affirmative defense of truth. The defendant, who had to plead truth as a defense in order to raise the issue, now has the burden of proving truth at the trial. This process will become clear as we read the trial transcript that follows.

Court stenographers generally record the complete trial, but unfortunately it is not customary to record the questioning of jurors. We can tell, however, from the opening statements of the attorneys, that the jurors were made aware of several aspects of this case during the "voir dire." At one point, for example, you will notice that Mr. Lisman indicates that he probably asked jurors if any of them was a deputy sheriff. We turn now to these opening statements.

Opening Statement by Mr. Louis Lisman:

May it please the Court, Ladies and Gentlemen of the Jury:

Well, I guess you already know this is a libel action and that the plaintiff is Mr. Towle and the defendant is the St. Albans Publishing Company. The St. Albans Publishing Company is a corporation up in St. Albans which publishes the St. Albans Daily Messenger. I guess by now none of this is new to you.

Now this much is undisputed, and some other things are undisputed, but before I go into that I want to tell you that what I say or what any lawyer says to you is not evidence. It doesn't make proof—it doesn't prove anything. The evidence will come from the witnesses as they answer the questions put to them. What I am going to say to you now is what Mr. Towle thinks and claims the evidence in this case will show. We are hoping the evidence will be brief. Unless we get involved in some remote things it probably will be brief, and we may be able to get you out of here by tonight.

Now on November 25, 1957, and again on November 26, 1957, these statements about which Mr. Towle complains were made. At that time Mr. Towle was a resident of Fairfax, up in Franklin County, within the St. Albans Messenger sphere. He was in the Air Force at the time and held a sergeant's rank and he was in line for promotion.

He also conducted a radio and television business in Fairfax, both repair work and selling them, and he had a pretty good business in which he was making $1,000 to $1,500 a year. Of course, it was a part-time business because he was in the Air Force, stationed here at the Base and this was a part-time business which brought him in a thousand to fifteen hundred dollars a year.

As I said before, he was sergeant and in line for promotion at the time. The promotion would have brought him another $50 increment in his pay if he had gotten the promotion.

Up in Franklin County at this time they had what was known as the sheriff's patrol. The sheriff of Franklin County had deputies. I probably asked you if any of you were a deputy sheriff. The sheriff up there had this sheriff's patrol and they used to patrol the highways and Mr. Towle was one of these special deputies.

Now on November 25, 1957, Mr. Towle had a driver's license issued in the State of Virginia. Before that, his right to drive had been suspended in the State of Vermont. He was brought into court up in St. Albans and charged with operating while under suspension and he pleaded guilty and paid a fine. The same evening, this paper comes out in the evening, the St. Albans

Daily Messenger comes out with the story that he had pleaded guilty to DWI, something altogether different. Well, he wasn't very happy about that. He called it to the attention of his superiors at the air force base and the next day the St. Albans Messenger printed another story. The first story, that he had been convicted of driving while intoxicated, appeared—we will have this as evidence for you—appeared on the inside page of the newspaper on page two. It was a paragraph in a story which told of about half a dozen—more than that—about eight or nine other cases. This next story, the next day, appeared on the front page of the Messenger right in here—the left-hand side. It was a long story, ran over on to page three and had two columns there at the top of page three. You would think in that story they would have taken back—

Mr. Mulvey: Excuse me for interrupting ． ． ．

Mr. Lisman: Oh, I am sorry, that isn't argument. I will take that back.

The Court: Mr. Lisman has withdrawn that statement.

Mr. Lisman: Yes, I am sorry, Your Honor. I got carried away.

The story the second day did not retract anything of what they said when they stated falsely he was convicted of driving drunk and instead it reported, which was true, that he had been convicted the previous day of driving under suspension, driving when his license was suspended, and then went on to say he had been dropped from the patrol, the sheriff's patrol, for misuse of authority. They went on to repeat that several times during the article. They hadn't withdrawn, you see, this story he had been convicted of drunken driving, didn't correct that, but in addition to telling the public he had been convicted of driving while under suspension they add that he had been suspended for misuse of authority. Now, Mr. Towle says that is false, and I believe the evidence will show that to be false.

Now, as a result of the publicity, particularly that he had been convicted of drunken driving, his customers up in Fairfax refused to do any more business with him in his radio and TV business. We will present evidence of that. One of them said he didn't want some day to get back his radio set or TV set and find, instead of a tube there was a beer bottle in it. We have a number of letters from his customers and there will be evidence of phone calls, and so forth, and as a result of that publicity, his radio and television business collapsed. Our evidence will show that he showed this second story to these people in Fairfax in order to convince them he had not been convicted of drunken driving and our evidence will show that they took the position that didn't change anything, that the story didn't say he was not convicted of drunken driving but apparently some additional offense had been committed. So he lost his business and the thousand or fifteen hundred dollars a year that went with it.

Our evidence will further tend to prove that he was made so uncomfortable in Fairfax on account of these stories that he sold out and moved away. He owned a home up there. He had put in about a thousand dollars of improvements, but he sold it for what he had paid for it. He lost his one thousand dollars in improvements so that was an additional loss to him.

The Air Force said because of this publicity he had had, particularly about—they knew he wasn't guilty of drunken driving—but particularly the story he had been suspended from the sheriff's patrol for misuse of authority, they didn't think he ought to get his promotion. So from that day in '57 until this in '59 he hasn't had any promotion, with the resulting pecuniary loss there. That is what we believe the evidence will show. We may be able to show it through a single witness and by documents, and if we can we will try to do it in order to save time. If not, we will produce additional witnesses. Thank you.

The Court: Mr. Mulvey, do you wish to make your opening statement at this time?

Mr. Mulvey: I do, if the Court please.

Opening Statement by Mr. Mulvey:

Ladies and Gentlemen, as Mr. Lisman has said, what I say isn't evidence. My job here now is to explain to you what our evidence will show with regard to the issues being raised in this case.

Our evidence we expect will show that a story was in fact published in the back pages of the newspaper in the court news, in the St. Albans Daily Messenger, stating this man pleaded guilty to driving while under the influence of intoxicating liquor and commonly referred to as DWI, and the fact of the matter was, and we will concede, that he was accused of and had pleaded guilty to the criminal offense of driving while his license was suspended.

Our evidence will show the reporter, the lady who took that information, inadvertently said DWI when she intended to put DWS. Our evidence will show that the paper, in an attempt to show what the true facts were, the next day reported that this man had been in court the day before and had pleaded guilty to driving while under suspension.

Now as to the balance of that story, our evidence will show that we published it in good faith, relying on what we considered good authority, and as far as we can determine, substantially, the story about the sheriff's patrol is correct. Our evidence we think will show that it is and it was published just as any other news story. Our evidence will show that the Air Force did order a discontinuance of its personnel taking part in the sheriff's patrol, which is part of that story and the elements in the second story were substantially as published in the paper.

As I said before, the first story inadvertently said DWI when it meant DWS and our evidence will show, at least we think the evidence will bear the inference it is a crime of similar nature, although it was an error and we tried to correct it.

That, in substance, I say is our position in the case and we think we will be able to back it up with sufficient evidence to convince you of the soundness of it. Thank you.

As these statements suggest, the function of the opening statement is to alert the jury to the nature of the case and to the lines of evidence to be presented. Note, however, that each attorney is careful to warn the jury that his statement is not itself evidence, but only his expectation of what the evidence will prove. Mr. Lisman set forth the substance of the claims and emphasized the damages he will try to show. Since the defendant has admitted the falsity of the first story, Mr. Lisman already knows that Sergeant Towle will be entitled to *some* damages, and his opening statement will encourage the jurors to think about damages from the outset. At one point, Mr. Mulvey breaks into Mr. Lisman's statement. What is this interruption all about?

The judge asks Mr. Mulvey whether he wishes to make his opening statement at this time because the defendant has a choice. Mr. Mulvey might have decided to wait until all of Mr. Lisman's evidence had been heard and then to make his opening statement just before presenting his own case. Most attorneys choose to make their opening statement as soon as possible, as did Mr. Mulvey, perhaps hoping to raise doubts that the jury will keep in mind while the plaintiff's evidence is presented.

Perhaps the most important point to observe in the opening statements is that they present nothing new. The attorneys spring no surprises. The pleadings and the pretrial conference have narrowed the issues, and the trial must be conducted within those bounds.

N. THE PLAINTIFF'S CASE

As the moving party in this litigation, it is the plaintiff's obligation to proceed first to his proof. He must be able to present evidence to support each disputed claim he has made in his pleadings. Having selected a legal theory justifying relief, Mr. Lisman has, in preparation for trial, collected whatever physical evidence and documents support his case and has decided which witnesses he wants to call. To assist him in this process, he is allowed to use the "subpoena" power to guarantee the appearance of essential witnesses and also to obtain essential documents. Quite literally, those who receive subpoenas will find themselves "under penalty" unless they comply.

There is frequently discussion about the extent to which the attorney may properly talk with witnesses before the actual trial. It is not only unethical to urge a witness to tell a false story; it is also a crime. The witness, who swears to tell the truth, will be committing perjury if he deliberately lies on the witness stand, and the attorney will be guilty of "subornation" or inducement of perjury. On the other hand, it is entirely proper, and desirable, for an attorney to review with a witness any prior statements the witness has made and to attempt to relieve the inevitable "stage fright" of inexperienced witnesses. The attorney may warn the witness about what kinds of questions he may be asked by both attorneys and may familiarize him with the procedures and help to jog his memory to recall as much as he can about the matters in question. Do you see the ethical dividing line?

O. THE PLAINTIFF TESTIFIES

An attorney will generally call upon only those witnesses he expects to provide favorable testimony. He is the first to question them, in a step called "direct" examination to distinguish it from the opposing attorney's questioning or "cross" examination. As you read this transcript of the testimony remember that the jurors have not yet heard any details of the case nor have they seen the pleadings, which are used only to determine the issues to be tried. They will learn about the case solely from the opening statements of the attorneys, the testimony, the closing statements, and the final comments of the judge. We turn now to Mr. Lisman's first witness, Sgt. Towle, whose first act was to take the prescribed witness' oath (12 V.S. § 5810):

> You solemnly swear that the evidence you shall give, relative to the cause now under consideration, shall be the whole truth and nothing but the truth. So help you God.

Ronald Towle Sworn. Direct Examination by Mr. Louis Lisman:

Q. Your name is—

A. Ronald W. Towle.

Q. You will have to talk up.

A. Ronald W. Towle.

Q. Are you in the military service at this time?

A. I am.

Q. In what branch?

A. I am in the United States Air Force.

Q. What is your rank?

A. Staff Sergeant.

Q. How long have you been staff sergeant in the service?

A. I have been staff sergeant for nine years.

Q. How long have you been in the service?

A. I have been in the service eighteen years.

Q. Where are you now stationed, Sergeant?

A. I am stationed in Newfoundland, Harmon Air Force Base.

Q. Have you come back here for the trial of this case?

A. I did.

Q. Where was your home at the time you brought this suit?

A. I was living in Milton.

Q. Now, were you in the service on November 25, 1957?

A. I was.

Q. Did you then have a rank of staff sergeant?

A. I did.

Q. Were you then in line for promotion?

A. I was.

Q. To what rank?

A. Next highest rank—tech sergeant.

Q. That is technical sergeant?

A. They just call it tech sergeant.

Q. Was there an increase in pay that would go along with that?

A. Yes, about fifty dollars a month.

Q. At that time where did you live?

A. At that time I lived in Fairfax.

Q. Was your family living there with you?

A. They were.

Q. Who was your family?

A. My wife and son.

Q. Were you conducting some business in Fairfax?

A. I was. Radio and television repair.

Q. By the way, does the Air Force permit you to do that?

A. They do.

Q. Did you conduct that as a full-time or part-time business?

A. As a part-time job.

Q. Will you tell us whether or not it was a profitable business?

A. Yes, sir, it was.

Q. How long had you been running this business in November, 1957?

A. I ran the business about a year—about a year and a half. Just about a year and a half.

Q. Had you been making money on it?

A. I was.

Q. Tell us how much you made per year?

A. The first year I made about a thousand dollars. The next year the business got a little better and I was making about fifteen hundred, I figured.

Q. So if your business had continued you would have made fifteen hundred dollars in that year?

A. Right.

Q. The year before you made a thousand dollars?

A. Yes.

Q. In your opinion, if business had continued—

Mr. Mulvey: We object to that. Certainly self-serving.

Mr. Lisman: All right, I will waive it.

Q. Where did you keep your business, did you have a store for it?

A. One side of my main house, I had a room where my shop was.

Q. Did you own your own home in Fairfax?

A. I did.

Q. How long had you owned your own home in Fairfax?

A. We bought that in '54.

Q. Did you make some improvements in your home?

A. I did.

Q. Will you tell us the cost, the total cost of those improvements?

A. Total cost was about fifteen hundred dollars.

Q. Did they increase the value of your property?

A. Yes, they did.

Q. By how much?

A. Oh, I should say about a thousand or fifteen hundred dollars more.

Q. Now, you conducted your business in some part of your house?

A. Yes, I did.

Q. Did you have any expenses in connection with your business other than purchase of parts and materials?

A. And power.

Q. And what?

A. Electric power and heat.

Q. So that those were all of your expenses in connection with that business?

A. Yes.

Q. The rest of what you took in was profit?

A. Right.

Q. Now, in 1957 did you have a license to drive a motor vehicle?

A. I did.

Q. Where was it issued?

A. Virginia.

Q. How did you happen to get a license in Virginia?

A. I was stationed in Virginia at that time.

Q. You got your license at that time?

A. Right.

Q. How long was it good for?

A. Four years.

Q. Virginia issues a license for four years at a time?

A. They do.

Q. Not one year at a time as in Vermont?

A. No. Four years at a time.

Q. How much time did you have to go on your Virginia license at that time?

A. Until December.

Q. December, 1957?

A. Right.

Q. Now, in November of 1957 then you still had a Virginia operator's license, is that right?

A. Right.

Q. Who was the sheriff of Franklin County?

A. Sheriff John Finn.

Q. Was he sheriff in November, 1957?

A. He was.

Q. Did he appoint you to some position or job?

A. Appointed me special deputy sheriff.

Q. What were your functions?

A. More or less highway patrol, what they call highway patrol, sheriff's patrol.

Q. In November, 1957, were you still a deputy sheriff?

A. 1957, yes, sir.

Q. In November?

A. Yes, I was.

Q. When did you cease to be a deputy sheriff?

A. Right after that, about a month after that, I think it was. Just about the same time in November.

Q. In November?

A. In November, right.

Q. You remember being in court?

A. I do.

Q. Were you still a deputy sheriff at that time?

A. At that time, yes.

Q. So you hadn't been at that time suspended from your office or anything?

A. No, I hadn't.

Q. Now, on November 25, 1957, you say you were in court in St. Albans, is that correct?

A. Right.

Q. And at that time did you plead guilty to the offense of driving while your license was suspended?

A. I did.

Q. At that time your Vermont license had been suspended, is that correct?

A. That's right.

Q. But your Virginia license was still in force, is that right?

A. That's right.

Q. But they fined you anyway?

A. They fined me anyway.

Q. Is there a newspaper in St. Albans called the Daily Messenger?

A. There is.

Q. Is that published by the St. Albans Publishing Company, Inc.?

A. It is.

Q. And does it come out evenings?

A. Yes, I believe it does.

Q. I show you a paper marked Plaintiff's 2 and ask you what that is?

A. Daily Messenger, Monday, November 25, 1957.

Q. That was the paper published the same day you were in court?

A. Right.

Q. And is that the paper marked Plaintiff's 2 on page two of the Messenger?

A. That's right.

Q. Will you look on page two of Plaintiff's 2 and tell us if there is a story there about you?

A. There is.

Q. Does that story appear in the third column?

A. It does.

Q. The third column, counting from the left?

A. From the left.

Mr. Lisman: We offer Plaintiff's 2, or rather that portion of Plaintiff's 2 on page two in which the head-line starts, "Arraign Nine", which is the third column.

Mr. Mulvey: We have no objection to the admission of that news story, Appears that is what it is.

The Court: Do counsel want to block that third column out? Block the side so it will be more readily available to the jury?

Mr. Lisman: I have done that, Your Honor.

The Court: Plaintiff's 2 may be admitted.

Q. I point to the sixth paragraph of the article in Plaintiff's Exhibit 2 which has been blocked out in pencil. Do you see that paragraph?

A. Right.

Q. Will you place a circle around it? Have you done that?

A. I have.

Q. Now I am going to read you what you circled and ask you what part of it is so and what part of it is not so—understand me?

A. Yes.

Q. "Ronald Towle of Fairfax, an air policeman," is that true?

A. True.

Q. "formerly of Enosburg"?

A. True.

Q. "pleaded guilty to driving while intoxicated", is that true?

A. Not true.

Q. Were you charged on November 25, 1957 of driving while intoxicated?

A. I was not.

Q. Or were you charged on November 25, 1957 of driving while under the influence of intoxicating liquor?

A. I was not.

Q. Have you ever been charged with DWI or driving while under the influence of intoxicating liquor?

A. I never have.

Q. Did you see this story when it was published in the newspaper?

A. I did.

Q. You had not been convicted of driving while intoxicated?

A. That's right.

Q. When did you see it?

A. I saw it that evening.

Q. Did you do anything about it?

A. I took it to my superiors in the air force.

Q. And do you know whether they got in touch with the St. Albans Messenger people?

    Mr. Mulvey: If the Court please, this certainly is going to be hearsay.

    Mr. Lisman: Yes, but it will save calling an extra witness who would only testify to one little thing.

    Mr. Mulvey: At least you can come up and tell us what.

    The Court: Yes, come to the Bench, please.

(Discussion off the record)

    The Court: You are going to withdraw the question?

    Mr. Lisman: Yes, I will withdraw the question in view of the fact it is objected to.

Q. Now, we have been talking about November 25, 1957. Did you see the St. Albans Messenger for November 26, 1957?

A. I did.

Q. Now this other story that we have been talking about, the one that falsely accused you of driving while intoxicated, appeared on the second page of the St. Albans Messenger, is that right?

A. That is right.

Q. The next day was there another story about you?

A. There was.

Q. Do you know what page that appeared on?

A. Started on the front page.

Q. I show you Plaintiff's 3 and ask you if that is the next day's newspaper?

A. That is.

Q. Does that story appear on the front page?

A. It does. Right here.

Q. And you are pointing to the first column from the left, is that right?

A. Right.

Q. Did the whole story appear on the front page?

A. No, it doesn't. It goes on to page three.

Q. It was continued on the third page?

A. That's right.

Q. Does the rest of it appear on the third page?

A. It does.

    Mr. Lisman: We offer Plaintiff's 3.

    Mr. Mulvey: As I understand, Plaintiff's 3 is the story that appears regarding the plaintiff here that appears on page one and page three— the story or the whole thing?

    Mr. Lisman: The story being referred to appears on page one and page three.

    Mr. Mulvey: I have no objection.

    The Court: Counsel care to block that off also? Plaintiff's 3 may be admitted.

Q. Now on November 25th the St. Albans Messenger reported that you had been convicted of driving while intoxicated, is that right?

A. That is true.

Q. And that story was false?

A. That is right.

Q. Now I show you Plaintiff's Exhibit 3, the St. Albans Messenger for the next day, November 26, 1957. Will you please read the story again that they wrote about you?

A. The whole thing or just the paragraph?

Q. No, read it to yourself.

    Mr. Mulvey: Is this necessary? This is in evidence now and they will have it.

    The Court: I think this is to refresh his recollection at the moment.

    Mr. Mulvey: Is that right?

    Mr. Lisman: Yes.

    Mr. Mulvey: I withdraw the objection.

Q. Sergeant, have you read that story again?

A. I have.

Q. Did you see anything in it that said you had not been convicted of DWI?

A. I did not.

Q. Did you see anything in it when you read it just now that took back any of the previous day's story, that you hadn't been convicted of DWI?

Mr. Mulvey: I think the item will have to speak for itself. That is what the jury is for. They will have these papers, if the Court please.

Mr. Lisman: The previous question covered the same ground.

The Court: Without objection.

Mr. Mulvey: Why go into it?

The Court: I think we will sustain the objection, Mr. Lisman.

Mr. Lisman: All right.

Q. I am going to read the story of November 26th to you and you tell me whether—which part is true and which part is not true. "A man who five months ago was suspended from the Franklin County Sheriff's Patrol"—were you suspended five months before from the Franklin County Sheriff's Patrol?

A. I was not.

Q. On the day of this article, November 26, 1957, or when you had appeared in court, had you yet been suspended?

A. I was not.

Q. It goes on to say you were "arraigned in municipal court here yesterday and pleaded guilty to driving for the past nine years on a suspended license"—is that true?

A. I did not.

Q. What did you plead guilty to?

A. I pleaded guilty to driving while under suspension on a technicality only.

Mr. Mulvey: If the Court please, the record will show for itself what he pleaded guilty to. I have the record in that particular hearing.

Mr. Lisman: He has a right to state what is true or not true, regardless of the record.

Mr. Mulvey: I think he has a right to answer the question what did he plead guilty to. He was going to continue on.

Mr. Lisman: Oh, yes, I think he was but I think we stopped him. He was going to say something else.

Q. To go on. "Ronald Towle of Fairfax"—was your home— is that correct?

A. Yes.

Q. They got that right. Were you from Fairfax?

A. Yes.

Q. So that is right. "Who was dropped from the patrol in June for misuse of authority"—were you dropped from any patrol for misuse of authority?

A. I was not.

Q. "—was brought before Municipal Court Judge Carl S. Gregg, and was fined $50, plus costs." Is that true?

A. I was brought before Judge Gregg, yes, that is true.

Q. —"A sergeant with the Air Police at the St. Albans Air Force Base," is that true?

A. True.

Q. —"the 36 year old native of Enosburg had his license suspended by the commissioner of motor vehicles in 1948, after he failed to file automobile liability insurance while he was overseas in the Army." True?

A. True.

Q. "State police said that Towle was convicted of careless and negligent driving, death resulting"—now going on to page three—"in St. Albans on May 19, 1941." Was that true?

A. It is true.

Q. "Troopers said a vehicle operated by him was involved in a fatal crash at Bakersfield. A passenger in the car was killed." Was that true?

A. True.

Q. "State police said he entered the armed service in 1943, and had his operator's license reinstated in 1946." Was that true?

A. Yes.

Q. "Two years later, troopers said Towle allowed his automobile liability insurance to lapse and his license was again suspended. Police said it has not been reinstated since." True?

A. True.

Q. "In court yesterday, the former deputy"—

A. I was still a deputy.

Q. —"reported having a Virginia license which is good for 4 years, and expires in 1958. Further, he said his car was fully insured." True?

A. That is true.

Q. "Judge Gregg, meanwhile, said today court records show that as a deputy, the 36-year-old airman was the arresting officer in six motor vehicle cases prosecuted here during the months of May, June and July."

A. True.

Q. "As a deputy, Towle was given a permit by the commissioner of public safety to equip his car with a siren and red warning lights." Is that true?

A. That is true.

Q. "His appointment as a deputy sheriff was made by Franklin County Sheriff John R. Finn, and was approved by the Attorney General of Vermont."

A. True.

Q. "Finn said this morning his commission as deputy and his permit from the department of public safety were withdrawn when he was dropped from the patrol for misuse of authority—", is that true?

A. Not true.

Q. —"and on order of the Office of Strategic Information, USAF, Ft. Ethan Allen, Vermont." Is that true?

A. That is true.

Q. At that time or some time did the air force adopt a policy that its men not serve as civilian enforcement officials?

A. They did.

Q. Is that when you dropped out of the patrol?

A. That is true.

Q. Did the air force notify various sheriffs, to your knowledge, of their new policy?

A. That I don't know.

Q. But you dropped out when they adopted this new policy?

A. I did.

Q. You noticed, did you, two or three references that you were dropped for misuse of authority?

A. I noticed them.

Q. Were they true?

A. Not true.

Q. You were appointed to the highway patrol by the sheriff of Franklin County?

A. True.

Q. With the approval of the Attorney General of Vermont?

A. Yes.

Q. And you had a right to use a siren and lights on your car?

A. Yes.

Q. You did make several arrests in your capacity as deputy?

A. I did.

Q. But the statement you were suspended for misuse of authority, is that true?

A. That is not true.

Q. Now after these stories appeared in the St. Albans Messenger, did you continue for a time with your radio and television business in Fairfax?

A. I did.

Q. Was there a lot of talk in Fairfax that you know of on account of these stories?

A. There was.

Q. And as a result of these stories did you get some telephone calls from people in the town?

A. I did.

Q. Did some people speak to you about them?

A. They did.

Q. Did you get some letters?

A. I did.

Q. I show you papers marked Plaintiff's 4, 5, 6, 7 and 8. I ask you if those are letters you received after these stories appeared in the newspaper?

A. They are.

Q. You understand that by "stories in the newspapers" I refer to Plaintiff's Exhibits 2 and 3?

A. I do.

Q. Those are the stories in the St. Albans Messenger of November 25th and 26th?

A. That is true.

Q. Were those letters written by residents of the town of Fairfax?

A. They were.

Q. I show you Plaintiff's 4. Was that written by a resident of the town of Fairfax?

A. This was.

Q. Were all these letters mailed to you? Did you receive them all in the mail?

A. I did.

Q. Do I have the envelopes here in my hand?

A. You have.

    Mr. Lisman: We offer Plaintiff's 4.

    Mr. Mulvey: We object to the offer on the grounds what it says in here may well be self-serving, on the ground it is strictly hearsay and certainly would be prejudicial. This is some personal letter from some unknown person, at least unknown to us. It is certainly hearsay, self-serving, many other evidentiary reasons why it shouldn't be admitted. I notice, further it doesn't refer to any particular story.

    The Court: Supposing we take this opportunity to declare a recess for lunch. Do you gentlemen feel that coming back at one-fifteen may help us to dispose of this earlier?

    Mr. Lisman: That is all right with us, Your Honor.

    Mr. Mulvey: All right with us. We are here.
                 (NOON RECESS)

    The Court: Do we have on the record, Mr. Lisman, your specific reason for the offer?

    Mr. Lisman: No. If the Court please, at this time, we offer Plaintiff's 4 for the purpose simply for showing the plaintiff lost business on account of the defendant's libel.

    Mr. Mulvey: I think you have our objection. First of all, we can't cross-examine on the contents of this letter. It is hearsay and self-serving.

    The Court: Objection sustained.

Q. Now, Sergeant, among your customers in Fairfax in your radio and TV business, did you have one by the name of Douglas C. Decker?

A. I did.

Q. Bernard Upton?

A. I did.

Q. Philip Parah?

A. I did.

Q. Did you have Mr. and Mrs. D. W. Decker among your customers?

A. Yes.

Q. Did you have Louis Brodeur among your customers?

A. I did.

Q. After the publication of the story in the St. Albans Messenger that you were convicted of driving drunk, did you get any business from these people?

A. I did not.

Q. Without telling us what they said, did they tell you why they wouldn't give you their business?

A. Yes, they did.

Q. Did they send you letters stating why they wouldn't give you their business?

A. Yes, they did.

Q. Are those the letters marked Plaintiff's 4, 5, 6, 7 and 8?

A. They are.

    Mr. Lisman: We again offer—we now offer Plaintiff's 4, 5, 6, 7 and 8 in connection with the witness's testimony, for the purpose of showing that the persons named by the witness in his testimony refused to give him their business.

    Mr. Mulvey: We object. On the same basis as on the first offer. I understand they are all the same. Strictly self-serving and we cannot cross-examine the people who are set forth here. The testimony has gone in and I don't see what these have to do but prejudice the jury.

    The Court: Objection sustained.

Q. Now, after you got these various letters, Plaintiff's 4, 5, 6, 7 and 8, did you talk with these people?

A. I did.

Q. Did you talk with them about the falsifications in the St. Albans Messenger stories?

A. I did.

Q. State whether or not you pointed out to them the second publication, Plaintiff's Exhibit 3, the one that appeared the second day?

A. Yes, I did. I pointed out to them the different charge—I mean the different charge instead of DWI, and deputy sheriff suspended from patrol, they thought that was just another charge added on to me.

    Mr. Mulvey: I don't believe he answered the question. It was not responsive.

    The Court: Let's have the question and answer read. You can make your objection then.

(Question and answer read)

    Mr. Mulvey: I don't think I understand the answer. May everything be stricken except "yes, I did"?

    Mr. Lisman: Yes.

    The Court: Yes, everything after "Yes, I did", may be struck.

Q. Please listen to the question and keep you voice up. Now, you say you showed these people the newspaper of the second day?

A. I did.

Q. Did you point out to them that the second day's newspaper charged that the conviction was for driving while under suspension?

A. I did.

Q. Did you point out to them the second day's newspaper did not show a conviction of driving drunk?

A. I did.

Q. What was the response?

    Mr. Mulvey: I object to any response. That would be strictly hearsay. We don't object to what he did or what he showed but what was the response is immaterial. What was their response is certainly awful broad.

    The Court: We will sustain the objection. If you can produce some citation, Mr. Lisman, as to your position we may reverse ourselves.

    Mr. Lisman: May we have an exception?

    The Court: You may.

Q. Were you able to convince these people that the charge was not one of DWI but—driving while intoxicated—but one of driving while your license was suspended?

A. I could not.

Q. This second publication was not able to convince them of that?

A. That is true.

Q. Now in addition to the business of the people whose names I have read, did you lose the business of other people in your television and radio business?

A. I did.

Q. Did these other people get in touch with you some way?

A. They called me on the telephone, and see me on the street.

Q. You have to keep your voice up.

A. They called me on the telephone and see me on the street.

Q. Did they tell you why they were refusing their business to you?

A. No, they said they rather have somebody else.

Q. Did they tell you why?

Mr. Mulvey: Either yes or no, the answer is.

A. No.

Q. Was there any discussion with these people of what was in the newspaper?

A. Yes.

Q. State whether or not they told you that what was in the newspaper had anything to do with your losing their business.

A. They said newspapers didn't print anything wrong. It must be true, what they put in there or they wouldn't put it in.

Q. Did they believe what was in the newspaper?

A. They did.

Q. Did they believe you had been convicted or pleaded guilty to driving drunk?

Mr. Mulvey: We object. This is an intelligent witness here who can answer direct questions, doesn't have to be led completely, certainly doesn't have to keep repeating testimony. What they believed or didn't believe certainly is not material here. I don't see how he can testify to it. I think counsel ought to be requested not to continually lead this witness.

The Court: We will sustain your objection, Mr. Mulvey. However, if you have an objection to the form in which Mr. Lisman is asking a question, make it at the time the question is asked and when I think he is to be warned about a line I would take care of it at that time.

Q. Will you please state what your customers told you was the reason that they didn't give you any more business?

A. The reason was they said that they would rather have somebody else, somebody that doesn't drink.

Q. Have you ever given these people any cause to believe that you drink?

A. I have not.

Q. Have you ever driven a car after you had been drinking?

A. No, sir.

Q. Do you know of any other source of information that you ever drove while you were drinking except in these publications in the St. Albans Messenger?

Mr. Mulvey: This is yes or no.

A. No.

Q. This is the only place where it was ever stated you had ever drunk or driven while you were drunk?

A. That is true.

Q. Now I think you told us before sometime this morning that you were in line for a promotion that was going to pay you how much?

A. It is $50. It is $50 a month between ranks.

Q. State whether or not you were about to get that promotion when this story came out?

A. I was up for the promotion at that one time.

Q. Did you get that promotion?

A. No, I didn't.

Q. Do you know the reason why you didn't get it?

Mr. Mulvey: Yes or no on it.

Q. Yes, just yes or no.

A. Yes.

Q. What was that reason?

Mr. Mulvey: If the Court please, I don't believe he can testify as to the reason.

Mr. Lisman: Who would know better?

Mr. Mulvey: The officers in his company could come in here and tell us why.

Mr. Lisman. You can call them but I prefer to get it from the witness.

Mr. Mulvey: Anything he can say would necessarily be self-serving, Your Honor. He is giving other people's reasons why he didn't get promoted, which those other people are in position to testify to, not him.

The Court: Objection sustained.

Mr. Lisman: May I have an exception?

The Court: Yes.

Mr. Lisman: I think I better make an offer on this at the Bench.

(At the Bench)

Mr. Lisman: We offer to show by this witness' testimony that the reason he did not get his promotion was that the newspaper, the St. Albans Daily Messenger in our exhibit 3, reported that he had been dropped from the highway patrol because of some sort of misconduct.

Mr. Lisman: While I am at the bench, I offered certain exhibits, 4 through 8, I believe, inclusive, which were excluded. Does the Court desire I make a further offer in connection with that? I want to have the Court understand the purpose of my offer.

The Court: I think the Court understood the purpose of your offer. The Court suggested that we would like some more on that admissibility counter to law which the Court researched this noon. If you had some we would be glad to see it.

Q. I guess we were through about your promotion when we interrupted and I think you told us you were in line for promotion. Was that in November, 1957?

A. That was.

Q. After these publications in the newspapers, in the St. Albans Messenger, you did not get your promotion, is that correct?

A. I didn't get it.

Q. Have you had your promotion since?

A. No, I haven't.

Q. From not getting it, you have lost the additional something like $50 a month?

A. That is true.

Q. What happened to your radio and television business?

A. I just had to give it up.

Q. Why did you have to give it up?

A. No business.

Q. Before these publications in the St. Albans Messenger, did you have business?

A. I had a good business.

Q. How much did you make from the business?

    Mr. Mulvey: If the Court please, counsel went all through this testimony this morning. We can be here for days if we keep going over and over.

    The Court: I think he may be laying additional foundation for something else. I may be wrong. I will let him proceed to see if that is the case. If it isn't, I will stop him.

Q. How much did you make from this business?

A. $1500.

Q. I think you told us in the first year you made—

A. $1,000 the first year and $1500—

Q. Keep your voice up. You are a sergeant and from all I have heard about sergeants they can keep their voices up. All right, now I show you these letters Plaintiff's 4, 5, 6, 7 and 8. Did you get them before or after these stories appeared in the St. Albans Messenger?

A. I got those after.

Q. A short time after or a long time after?

A. Short time after.

Q. Did these letters have anything to do with your closing down your business?

A. I never got any more business from them.

Q. Just answer my questions, please.

A. Yes.

Q. In what way?

A. Well, I just—they just said they didn't want any more business doing—that is the whole thing.

Q. How long after these stories appeared in the St. Albans Messenger did you remain in the town of Fairfax?

A. I believe around six months.

Q. Then what did you do?

A. I sold my place and moved into Milton.

Q. Were you able to sell your radio and TV business?

A. No, I wasn't. I just gave stuff away except my test equipment and tubes and things like that.

Q. Some of these things you still have?

A. I still have.

Q. But you don't do any more business?

A. I don't.

Q. You say you sold your place, is that what you said?

A. I did.

Q. What do you mean by that?

A. I sold my house.

Q. Why did you leave Fairfax?

A. To get away from all the ridicule I had around there.

Q. Where was that ridicule coming from?

A. From the papers.

Q. How about the newspaper report that you pleaded guilty to driving under suspension, did that bother any?

A. Nobody believed it. They just kept hollering, "Here comes the old drunk."

Q. Did they call you any other names?

A. I wouldn't want to mention some of them.

Q. Did they all have to do with drinking?

A. Most of them, yes.

Q. Did the newspaper story about your being dropped for misuse of authority from the highway patrol, did that cause people to call you names?

A. Yes, because they thought I was being drunk on highway patrol too.

Q. It was all related to this?

A. The whole thing.

Q. And as a result you moved away from Fairfax?

A. I did.

Q. You sold your home?

A. I did.

Q. What did you pay for your home when you bought it?

A. Four thousand.

Q. What was it worth when you bought it?

A. Worth about four thousand.

Q. Did you do any work to it after you bought it?

A. I did.

Q. I guess you told us about that this morning.

A. I did.

Q. How much do you say that work increased the value of the property?

A. Around $1500.

Q. What did you sell the property for?

A. $4500.

Q. So you sold it for about $500 more than you paid for it?

A. I did.

Q. You got back about only $500 of the $1500 increase in value?

A. That's right.

Q. If you had waited longer—

Mr. Mulvey: If the Court please, "If you had waited longer" —I object to the form of the question right off.

The Court: You are withdrawing the question, Mr. Lisman?

Mr. Lisman: I will withdraw the question and ask it again.

Q. Why didn't you wait longer before selling this property?

A. I just wanted to get out of there and get away from them.

Q. What was the property really worth—the property you sold for $4500—what was it really worth when you sold it?

Mr. Mulvey: He has already testified to that twice.

Mr. Lisman: We don't have a figure.

The Court: We will take the answer. Go ahead.

A. $5500.

Q. Now, besides the people in the town of Fairfax, were there other people that you knew that heard about the St. Albans Messenger story that you were convicted of drunken driving?

A. Yes.

Q. Who were these other people? I don't mean mention their names, but in general.

A. Just more or less general people I have known a short time, that I fixed TVs for out around.

Q. How about the people in your outfit in the service?

A. I wasn't too good there either.

Q. Did they hear about it?

A. They sure did.

Q. Did they have anything to say about it to you?

A. Just a lot of razzing.

Q. Subjected you to ridicule?

A. They did.

Mr. Lisman: You may examine.

Note on Direct Examination of Sergeant Towle

As the transcript indicates, there are some types of questions an attorney may not ask his own witness. Generally these questions fall into two categories: improper form and improper substance.

Sgt. Towle might have responded to a request for an unstructured narrative, "Please tell us in your own words the nature of your grievance," but he cannot be expected to know what is legally important and what is not. A general narrative answer might omit important things that the lawyer would still have to ask about and it would include much that is legally irrelevant or inadmissible.

Although attorneys are allowed to guide the course of the testimony by a succession of fairly limited questions about specific facts, these questions will be improper if they "lead" the witness by suggesting to him the answer desired by the attorney. Such phrases as "Isn't it true that" prompt the witness instead of eliciting what he remembers seeing or hearing or doing. You will notice that Mr. Lisman does this several times in the transcript but that Mr. Mulvey makes no objection. This is because most of the objectionable questions are formal in nature and leading questions will help speed the process along. Examples of this are such questions as "Is there a newspaper in St. Albans called the Daily Messenger?", and "Is that published by the St. Albans Publishing Company, Inc.?" While theoretically these questions are leading, they do help to speed the proceedings. Later, however, when the questions become important, Mr. Mulvey does object and the objections are sustained.

The other major limitation on form is that the questions must not be "argumentative." They must seek to elicit new facts rather than seeking the witness' assent to the attorney's interpretation of evidence already presented. The attorney may draw inferences from the evidence after all the testimony is in but not during the questioning itself.

You will notice that some of Mr. Mulvey's other objections did not go to the form of the question, but rather went to their substance. Generally, the witness is asked to recall his perceptions of a prior event: what he saw, or heard, and how he reacted. The law of evidence seeks to keep the case in focus through the concept of "relevance." Although the jury might be interested in learning where Sgt. Towle went to school and whether he likes classical music, these questions are irrelevant to the case. Occasionally, even relevant evidence is excluded because it is too time-consuming or because there is a substantial risk that it will mislead or confuse the jury. For example, if a woman is suing a bus company for closing the door on her foot as she was getting out, would you think it relevant that the woman's sister and aunt had made similar complaints against the same bus company five times before, but had lost every case? The fear is that a juror might think it so relevant that he might fail to give this woman a "fair trial" on the sixth case—and this might be the one in which it really happened. The evidence in the sixth case must concern only that particular episode without regard to the prior history of the plaintiff's relatives.

Why is a lawyer required to object at once to inadmissible evidence? Why can't he wait until the end of the trial to review the transcript at leisure and decide whether erroneous evidence has been admitted? However weighty the reasons, the rule is clear that objections must be made. The party adversely affected by the judge's ruling on an objection may challenge that ruling on appeal. Although it is now rarely necessary to demand an "exception" lawyers still say it as a matter of habit. Most of Mr. Mulvey's objections in this case deal with something called "hearsay"—probably the most significant substantive objection. The hearsay rule excludes testimony about statements made out of court by others that a party seeks to introduce in order to substantiate assertions he has made. Mr. Lisman wants the letters admitted to support Towle's assertions about why he lost customers. Mr. Mulvey wants them excluded because he cannot question those who wrote them to explore their motivations or to challenge their credibility. The letters could be introduced to show that on a certain date Sgt. Towle had received mail, but their contents could not be admitted to prove the truth of statements made in the letter.

The hearsay rule, however, has dozens of exceptions, and a moment's reflection will indicate why. For example, how can Sgt. Towle prove how old he is, or who his true parents are? He can know these things only by hearsay. Yet, if he were required to support each of these facts by first-hand knowledge a simple trial would become a protracted nightmare. Therefore, hearsay testimony may be presented where the evidence is so *reliable* and so *necessary* that, on balance, the denial of cross-examination is the lesser of the evils.

So much, then, for the basic rules of evidence. You will note that throughout the trial Judge Hill sits quietly and waits for the opposing attorney to "make an objection." Indeed, the judge tells Mr. Mulvey as much in an exchange in which the judge implies that there were earlier objectionable questions that he saw, but did not raise. It is unethical for an attorney to ask deliberately improper questions, and there is no reason whatever to think that either attorney in this case did so. Nevertheless, the rules of evidence are complicated and Mr. Lisman's questioning was probably not prepared verbatim in advance. It is only natural, then, to expect that certain questions will come up that will be improper either in form or in substance. If the judge alone realizes this, why shouldn't he reject the question? The answer to this goes to the very basis of our "adversary system." Indeed, if you think back, this problem has been with us throughout the case. Should a court intervene to tell an attorney that a better complaint can be written than the one he is using? Or that he should call a particular witness? Or ask him a specific question? The following excerpt discusses these questions.

CIVIL PROCEDURE

By Fleming James, Jr.

3–7 (1965).

A leading characteristic of the Anglo-American procedural system is its adversary nature. In civil disputes it is generally up to the parties, not the court, to initiate and prosecute litigation, to investigate the pertinent facts, and to present proof and legal argument to the tribunal. The court's function, in general, is limited to adjudicating the issues submitted to it by the parties on the proof presented by them, and to applying appropriate procedural sanctions upon motion of a party.

It will be noted that two separate principles are involved in the above statement—the principle of party-presentation and the principle of party-prosecution. The former concerns "content of the cause," the latter "the going forward of the cause." It should also be noted that while the Anglo-American legal system has traditionally allocated both of these roles largely to the parties, there is no inherent necessity that they march together in this way. It would be perfectly possible to give the parties control over the content of the cause to be decided but to provide that "once an action has come into being, the court, with or without motion, will cause to be taken all steps necessary for its adjudication." This is substantially the German civil system and . . . is coming increasingly to mark our own.

The adversary system also presupposes . . . "the principle of bilaterality"—that opportunity be given to both sides to investigate and to present proof and legal argument.

The principle of party-presentation represents in part a judgment that private parties should be masters of their rights under what is generally thought of as private law, that it is up to them to press or to waive claims or defenses, and that the social interest in securing general observance of the rules of private law is sufficiently served by leaving their enforcement to the self-interest of the parties more or less directly affected.

But the principle of party-presentation . . . is more intimately concerned with the relative roles of the *parties* and the *court*, and of course the court is just one agency of the public. Even if some civil rights are so important to society that it should take an active part in securing their enforcement, the decision to initiate and carry on investigation of suspected violations need not be vested in the courts—it can be and usually is vested in some other agency of society. Criminal law is largely administered on such a basis in this country, and so are many segments of the law in which administrative agencies are charged with the duty to investigate and then, if need be, to seek civil sanctions in the courts. Thus the adversary system and party-presentation may well exist in areas extensively regulated by government in what is deemed to be the public interest. Their existence stems not from laissez faire or a philosophy of individualism but rather from a notion of the proper allocation of function between the parties to a dispute (one of whom may be the government) and the tribunal which is to decide it, under any economic or social order, at least in a free society.

This other aspect of the adversary system and party-presentation represents two judgments: (1) that truth is more likely to emerge from bilateral investigation and presentation, motivated by the strong pull of self-interest, than from judicial investigation motivated only by official duty; and (2) that the moral force and acceptability of a decision will be greatest where it is made by one who does not have, and does not appear to have, the kind of psychological commitment to the result that is implied in initiating and conducting the investigation of a case. Involvement in the work of presenting each side of a case effectively is even more clearly inconsistent with the integrity of the adjudicative process.

On the other hand, little or no threat to this integrity seems likely to result from the court's taking an active role in moving the case along—expediting it—toward final decision. This would not seriously impair the adversary nature of investigation and presentation of cases or the parties' control over the content of the issues submitted to the court.

Moreover, the common law tradition is strong that the judge who conducts the trial should play an active part in directing it so that, within the issues made by the parties, the true facts of claims and defenses will emerge and the appropriate law be applied to them. To this end he could exercise considerable initiative. In nineteenth-century America, however, there was a strong movement to reduce the role and authority of the judge to that of mere umpire and to enlarge the sphere of the jury and the ability of the parties to play upon that body with a minimum of judicial interference. This was part of the notion of democracy of that era but it is not, it is submitted, an essential part of the adversary system. Nor does it tend to promote the values which the adversary system is aimed at preserving. The moral acceptability of a decision is not lessened or compromised by the judge's taking an active part during the proceedings to elicit the truth by suggesting the calling of additional witnesses. . . . The integrity of adjudication is not threatened by the court's examination of witnesses when their examination by the parties leaves stones unturned,

. . .

. . .

The tendency of modern American procedure is away from the extreme position which would render the judge a passive umpire . . . —and this is probably a good thing. The adversary system has faults as well as virtues. It brings forth guile and concealment as well as truth. It presupposes equality of opportunity, means, and skill; but these are seldom evenly matched.

It often degenerates into trial by combat with victory to the swift and strong rather than to the party in the right. Anything that the law of procedure or the judge's role can do to equalize opportunity and to put a faulty presentation on the right track so that disputes are more likely to be settled on their merits, will in the long run bolster up rather than destroy the adversary system, and will increase the moral force of decisions.

. . .

Notes and Questions

1. What distinction does Professor James draw between the role of adversaries in initiating and framing the case and their role in conducting the case?

2. Assuming that each litigant can get an attorney, some inequalities of representation might be that one litigant has more money and can afford a battery of lawyers while the other can afford only a single attorney; that one lawyer is brighter and more creative than his adversary; or that an attorney may be inept in the sense of not knowing enough to object to improper questions. Are these equally serious problems?

3. Money can buy many things in our society including better medical treatment as well as better lawyers. Should the government do anything about this? What could it do?

4. If you think the judge should interfere at all, when should he do so? Do you see any dangers to the adversary system in judicial intervention?

Although during the trial parties must generally rely on their attorneys, a client may have a remedy against a careless lawyer. If a client believes he lost his case because of his attorney's carelessness—not merely debatable judgment about strategy—he may sue his attorney for what is called "professional negligence" or "malpractice." Many attorneys are insured against liability for such lapses. Even if such a suit succeeds, which is rare, it does not affect the initial judgment in favor of the opposing party but merely gives the loser redress against his own lawyer. Would it make more sense to alter the result in the original case?

Note that Judge Hill calls a noon recess without ruling on Mr. Mulvey's objection. For most routine questions the judge will have the rule at his fingertips; in unusual situations he may not. He also knows that if he makes a serious mistake, the whole case may have to be tried again. There was every reason to be cautious and this was a good time to take a recess.

Notice that the judge announced later that he had researched the question during the recess.

Mr. Lisman also had in mind the possibility of an appeal. His request for an "exception," and his "offer of proof" both seek to show an appellate court where he thinks Judge Hill erred and also what he would have been able to show had the judge allowed him to do so.

We may turn now to Mr. Mulvey's cross-examination.

———

Cross Examination by Mr. Mulvey:

Q. Mr. Towle, you were 18 years, did you say, in the service?

A. Right.

Q. You are still in the service, is that right?

A. Right.

Q. When you went into the service, these were not 18 continuous years, were they?

A. All but about six months.

Q. When was the last time you were out for any length of time?

A. Just let me see . . . 1956.

Q. And you joined the service then as what, corporal, was it?

A. Staff sergeant.

Q. When you joined the service after World War II you were a corporal?

A. Right.

Q. And then you rejoined in 1956?

A. Right. In the Air Force.

Q. Before that what branch were you in?

A. I was in the Army.

Q. In 1956 you joined the Air Force, is that correct?

A. Right. April, 1956.

Q. And then in April 1956 to April—this happened in April '57, that you were in court on a driving under suspension charge, right?

A. April?

Q. I mean November, 1957?

A. November '57, right.

Q. Where were you prior to April 1956?

A. I was with the National Guard.

Q. Did you have that business of repairing television sets at that time?

A. I did.

Q. Now you stated this morning that you had this business which gave you a return of about $1500?

A. That's right, one year.

Q. Do you have any tax records to show that particular figure or figures, substantially?

A. I do.

Q. Have you got them with you?

A. No, I haven't.

Q. Could you bring them in?

A. No.   They are in Newfoundland.

Q. What other records do you have—do you have federal and state income tax figures, both?

A. Yes, I do.

Q. When this happened you were staff sergeant, were you?

A. Right.

Q. And you are still staff sergeant?

A. Right.

Q. You stated on direct examination that everything was correct about the first newspaper story—that is, the newspaper story of November 25th—except that it said driving while intoxicated while it should have said driving while under suspension?

A. Should have said driving while under suspension, yes.

Q. But you were in court that day?

A. Yes.

Q. And you did plead guilty?

A. Right.

Q. The only thing wrong was the charge that they had in the paper, that was different than the charge you pleaded to, is that correct?

A. That is correct.

Q. I show you a paper marked Defendant's Exhibit A, which purports to be a certified copy of a complaint charging you with C & N driving. Look it over and tell me whether or not this is the fact, that you were in—

Mr. Lisman: Just a moment.

Mr. Mulvey: This has been admitted in the case by pre-trial conference.

The Court: The Court has one problem at this point, Mr. Mulvey. You might tell us the time. The Court can't recall any testimony that in 1956—

Mr. Mulvey: 1957.

The Court: '57 that there was a C & N?

Mr. Lisman: May we come to the Bench?

The Court: Yes.

(Discussion off the record)

Mr. Mulvey: Excuse me, I meant to say driving under suspension.

The Court: That makes an entirely different situation.

Q. You are a deputy sheriff, you have brought people into court, you know what a driving under suspension charge is?

A. Right.

Q. Will you look this over and see if you recall that?

A. I recall this.

Mr. Lisman: Keep your voice up.

A. I do recall this.

Mr. Mulvey: This is an exhibit which is the record of that day, November 25, 1957.

Q. Now on direct testimony, Mr. Towle, you stated that you had read the paper on the 26th. Now you stated that it was true that you were a sergeant, that it was true that you had failed to file automobile liability insurance, that it was true you were driving on a Virginia automobile operator's license?

A. Right.

Q. It was true you had been convicted previously of C & N driving, death resulting, is that right?

A. That is right.

Q. Now you stated then that as a result of the newspaper publications, the part you state was not true, that you suffered this loss of business, is that right?

A. That is right.

Q. Now the sections here that say you were convicted of—that you admit to be true—careless driving, death resulting, you testify that had nothing to do with your loss of business, is that right?

A. That is right.

Q. Your feeling is people will—people particularly who talked to you, in effect said, We don't mind a conviction of C & N, death resulting but the charge of intoxication while driving or driving while under the influence is what bothered them?

A. Right.

Q. Did they tell you why this death charge was not important but the other one was?

A. I didn't have my business then.

Q. But you had your business when they found out you were the same man, didn't you?

A. Right.

Q. Do you know whether or not—did you tell the sheriff you had been so convicted when he hired you as deputy?

A. I don't remember.

Q. You probably did not—

Mr. Lisman: Just a moment. First of all I didn't hear the question.

Mr. Mulvey: I will withdraw the question.

Q. Now in connection with this charge which you admit is true, C & N, death resulting, it was the initial time you were suspended, is that right?

A. Right.

Q. You were sentenced to State's Prison, weren't you?

Mr. Lisman: Just a moment, just a moment. I object to any evidence of sentence.

Mr. Mulvey: I think it is perfectly proper.

The Court: Gentlemen, could I see you at the Bench.

(At the Bench)

The Court: Have all the grounds of your objection you want to make, Mr. Lisman, been put on the record?

Mr. Lisman: As far as this particular question is concerned.

The Court: As far as this particular question is concerned, I will exclude this question. I think the first question, however, is in and will stay in. I will not take the second question though, Mr. Mulvey. That is an entirely different matter.

Mr. Mulvey: In other words, I have asked if he was sentenced to State's Prison. That is excluded. Now, first of all, this is a party, not only a witness. Second, this is cross-examination of a party. Third, this whole story in the paper was put into evidence by this party which concerned this particular charge I am questioning on.

The Court: The Court thinks you have questioned him far enough on that charge and as far as this particular question is concerned, we will exclude it.

Mr. Mulvey: May I ask the question again so it will be clear?

Q. You were in Court as stated in the paper sometime previous to this on a charge of careless and negligent driving, death resulting, is that right?

A. Right.

Q. You were on that particular charge sentenced, is that correct?

A. No.

Mr. Lisman: He is doing the same thing.

Mr. Mulvey: No, not yet.

The Court: The witness has answered the question. Do you still want to renew your objection, Mr. Lisman?

Mr. Lisman: Yes, Your Honor. May my objection be treated as timely, Your Honor, and the answer stricken.

The Court: We will have the answer stricken, Mr. Mulvey.

Q. I want to get this straight. If the record were to show that you were in—

Mr. Lisman: Just a moment. This is the same thing over and over. We object to it.

The Court: Let's not have argument, it sounds like closing argument here. Do you want to come to the Bench and tell us what this is all about?

(At the Bench)

> Mr. Mulvey: The question regarding the State's Prison sentence resulting from the conviction of C & N, death resulting, is to show the fact that he was sentenced to State's Prison, the sentence was suspended, and it is offered among other things in mitigation of damages.

> The Court: We will exclude the pending question.

Q. Now, as a deputy sheriff, your reputation suffered a little bit when you were in court, is that right?

A. It did.

Q. If you were in court on any charge it would have had some effect, you agree?

A. Why, yes.

Q. And if you had been in court on a charge of driving while your license was suspended, you would still have had to explain a little bit to your friends, is that right?

A. That's right.

Q. Now, some time previous to the time you were in court the Air Force issued an order, didn't they, regarding deputy sheriffs?

A. They did.

Q. That was before the 25th day of November when you were in court?

A. That's right.

Q. So the Air Force issued their order which in substance stated you could not any longer be a deputy sheriff?

A. That's right.

Q. Then at the time you were in court, either you were in compliance with the order of the Air Force and no longer acting as deputy or you were contrary to that order, one or the other?

A. Yes.

Q. At the time you were in court on that charge, you were, I assume, as a good soldier, complying with that order?

A. That's right. I wasn't on patrol.

Q. So you hadn't been acting as a deputy for some time?

A. I don't remember when I quit.

Q. You quit as soon as you got that order, didn't you?

A. That's right, I don't know the date.

Q. It might be fair to say you were not acting as deputy when you were in court on the charge of driving while under suspension?

A. Right.

Q. Now when you testified you were a deputy at that time, you must have misunderstood?

A. It could have been.

Q. Now, you were in court on November 25th. Some time previous to that—

Mr. Mulvey: Just to refresh the witness's recollection I want to show him a paper. Will you mark it for identification, please?

Q. Now one of the things stated in the paper was that you had been suspended from the sheriff's patrol for misuse of authority, is that right?

A. That's right.

Q. In connection with that particular item I want you to look over this letter that is from the Department of Public Safety, signed by Commissioner Baumann. Just to refresh your memory.

A. That's right.

Q. Did you receive a copy of it?

A. I did.

Q. Some time in connection with your duties as a deputy sheriff, sometime in May, 1957, did you go to Waterbury?

A. I did.

Q. And at the time you were driving your automobile?

A. I was.

Q. And you had your siren and your red light on?

A. Yes, I did.

Q. Was a complaint—to your knowledge was a complaint made regarding your actions as a deputy to the sheriff in Franklin County?

Mr. Lisman: Your Honor, I object. That has nothing to do with the libel made in the newspapers.

Mr. Mulvey: It has to do with the misuse of authority element that is in the case.

Mr. Lisman: No, whether a complaint was made is only hearsay.

The Court: As I remember the framing of this question
it is directed to his own knowledge, which
takes it, I would think, away from hearsay.
And on the offer of Mr. Mulvey that it goes
to the matter of misuse of authority, we will
allow it subject to being tied completely into
that, and you may renew your objection if it
isn't, Mr. Lisman.

Q. Will you answer the question.

A. What was the question?

(Question read)

Mr. Lisman: That is, to his knowledge.

The Court: Yes.

A. Yes.

Q. The complaint I mean concerned your use of the light and
siren in town of Waterbury?

A. That was it.

Q. In connection with that complaint you received a notifica-
tion from the Department of Public Safety, is that right?

A. I did.

Q. And this was in May of 1957?

A. That's right.

Q. Now during this same—during the time that you were deputy, I should say, during the year 1957, there came a time
when in connection with your duties as deputy you transferred your siren and light to another car, is that right?

A. That's right.

Q. Did you do that with permission?

A. Yes, well it isn't permission. I had my permit. I didn't
know you had to renew the permit to put lights and siren
from one vehicle to another until the sheriff told me
that.

Q. In other words, it is fair to say the complaint also inti-
mated you had acted improperly in your duties as deputy
sheriff.

A. No, I didn't have no complaint then.

Q. Let's put it this way, were you not informed by proper
authorities that you had acted improperly—

Mr. Lisman: I object to the question.

Q. — as a deputy sheriff, in this regard?

The Court: Your grounds, Mr. Lisman?

Mr. Lisman: On the grounds it is hearsay.

Mr. Mulvey: I asked, was he informed.

Mr. Lisman: I asked if he was informed whether complaint had been made by the air force base to the St. Albans Messenger which you objected to and it was excluded. This is the same thing.

Mr. Mulvey: Our answer states the substantial truth of the publication of the 26th of November—

The Court: We will exclude it anyway.

Q. So you say it would be on this particular time, referring to the time on May 28, 1957, when you went to Waterbury, and would you explain to us what happened on that occasion?

A. I went to Waterbury to apprehend a man and bring him back for court. And going down I had two other fellows with me. The reason—we had to get there before they went off work and they didn't send us down until late and I blew the siren and had the red light on for safety factors only.

Q. Then you went, according to the letter which you said you received, you turned in to a restaurant?

A. Right. We had to stop there to make a phone call back to the sheriff's department.

Q. Then you would say in all fairness that there was at least a couple of complaints made to the sheriff about your actions—whether justified or not, complaints were made?

A. Only one.

[Apparently Mr. Lisman stood up and was about to object.]

The Court: We will take the answer. Again, subject to being tied into this one problem, Mr. Lisman.

Mr. Mulvey: Think the answer was yes.

Q. This complaint that you admit to and you admit there was another occasion when you transferred your lights without knowledge of the Department on Public Safety?

A. It is all on that one, right there. It came in all together.

Q. But there were two of them?

A. Right.

Q. You admit these things took place before you were in court, before the 25th of November.

A. Yes, that's right.

Q. Now, when was the last time you were out on patrol before November 25th, do you remember?

A. No, I don't.

Q. Could it have been—well, September?

A. I don't know. I don't remember when the last time was that I was out.

Q. Now, when you were on sheriff's patrol you state you had a Virginia license?

A. Right.

Q. What was your car registration, Virginia?

A. Vermont.

Q. And you were driving in Vermont with a Virginia license for four years or three years?

A. No. Just had a few months more to go to get a Vermont license.

Q. How long had you been using a Virginia license?

A. In Vermont? Just about a year then, something like that.

Q. Your car was registered in your name?

A. It was.

Q. Did there come a time when the sheriff informed you that you couldn't use your siren or light for a while until your new permit came back?

A. Right after this.

Q. Right after the Waterbury incident?

A. Right.

Q. So is it only on two occasions then you were in court? First, on this C & N, death resulting, and secondly on this driving while under suspension charge, is that right?

A. That is the only two times.

Q. Now there was a time when you lived in Enosburg, right?

A. Yes.

Q. You own a house in Enosburg?

A. Yes, I do now.

Q. And at the time you sold the house in Fairfax you purchased a house in Enosburg?

A. That's right.

Q. So you bought this house in Enosburg and you still own it, is that right?

A. That's right.

Q. So one of your reasons for selling, among others—always numerous reasons—among others, was to acquire the house in Enosburg?

A. Not necessarily.

Q. One of them? One of many?

A. It could be one of many.

Q. So it is fair to say you sold one house in one town in Franklin County and you bought another one?

A. Right.

Q. This second house you still own?

A. Right.

Q. There came a time, Mr. Towle, when you were transferred apparently to Newfoundland?

A. That's right.

Q. When was that?

A. A year ago the 6th of September.

Q. Now it is customary or let's say it is quite usual for a fellow to be in Vermont a couple years, then transfer overseas for a year or so and then back to the States? It is policy?

A. It is possible.

Q. It is policy usually, isn't it? Now, when was it you said you left the United States?

A. A year ago the 6th of last September.

Q. There is nothing to hinder you from having a television business in Newfoundland, is there?

A. Yes. It is against government regulations.

Q. But it is not against government regulations in the United States, is that it?

A. That's right.

Q. So even had this not occurred, I mean this mistake, for lack of a better term, you couldn't be doing anything over there as regards repairing TV, is that correct?

A. Not over there, no.

Q. How long had you lived in that house, Mr. Towle, before you sold it—and I am referring now to the Fairfax house?

A. '54, I think it was.

Q. 1954?

A. 1954.

Q. And you sold it in what year—what was the date?

A. '58.

Q. '58. Now, was it immediately that you bought this other house or did you wait awhile?

A. No, I bought it about the same time that I sold the other.

Q. Now you had lived there for three or four years, right?

A. In Fairfax.

Q. In Fairfax. And you got for the house $500 less than you had put into it?

A. Nearer a thousand.

Q. You said you put $1500 into it?

A. Right. I bought it for $4,000, put in $1500 and sold it for $4500. That leaves $1,000.

Q. You had lived there continually all the time?

A. Yes.

Q. I mean, you were stationed here. Your family had been living there all that time?

A. Yes.

Q. Why is it, Mr. Towle, you can say this publication, and I am referring to the story, the newspaper stories—this one of the 25th—mistakenly said DWI when it should have said driving under suspension, caused you all the trouble, when the one that had it you were in court for C & N, death resulting didn't cause you any trouble?

A. You have one, but the other one with it makes it that much worse.

Q. But the other one, except for your claim of non-misuse of authority, is true.

A. What do you mean?

Q. The other story, the story of the 26th, was substantially correct except for that item that says misuse of authority.

A. Most of it.

Q. But yet you say that one never bothered anybody, but the first one did?

A. I didn't say that one never bothered anybody. I said taking them both together, that makes it that much worse.

Q. You are a career man, aren't you, in the Air Force?

A. Right.

Q. And your intention, for all we know, is to continue on?

A. Yes.

Q. You have lived in Franklin County most of your life, haven't you?

A. Right.

Q. How long did you live in Milton?

A. Three or four months. I believe it was something like that, I don't remember exactly.

Q. Did you ever live in the Enosburg house you purchased?

A. Three months before I went overseas.

Q. So when you went overseas you were back living in Enosburg?

A. Just getting my family set.

Q. Your family still there?

A. No. They are in Newfoundland now.

Mr. Mulvey: I have no more questions . . . Before Mr. Lisman starts I want to ask him a few more. Something slipped my mind.

Q. Now since you stated on your direct examination that this story hurt you in the service, you thought it had anyway?

A. I thought it had, yes.

Q. But since November of 1957 isn't it true you have continued to receive recognition by the service? For example, were you not Airman of the Month in January of 1958?

A. Right. I wasn't Airman of the Month. They put the story in the paper about me to try to straighten up what had already happened.

Q. They put that in the paper, that you were Airman of the Month?

A. I don't know Airman of the Month or not. I know they put something in the paper.

Q. Any complaints on that story?

A. No.

Q. Your picture was on the front page and this particular story said you were a credit to the Air Force, that's true, isn't it?

A. True.

Q. This was after this publication in November?

A. That's right.

Q. It said you had won various awards as, it said, pistol expert?

A. Right.

Q. And this story appeared in the Messenger?

A. Yes.

Q. When you said they put that story in the paper to try to straighten things out, do you mean the Messenger?

A. No, the Air Force.

Q. So your picture appeared in the paper with a story about how good you were, is that right?

A. Right.

Q. Nothing incorrect that time—no mistakes as far as you could determine?

A. No. Didn't read it that close.

Q. So when they said you were Airman of the Month, received an award as Airman of the Month, that wasn't true? Said that you were recognized by the Air Force?

A. That's what the special service officer said. I don't know about the rest.

Q. That was true then?

A. That was true.

Mr. Mulvey: That is all.

Notes on Cross-Examination of Sgt. Towle

One of the underlying premises of the adversary system, as we have seen, is that truth is more likely to emerge from the strong pull of self-interests than from a "neutral" investigation by a government official. This is especially relevant at the trial stage where the "truth" is being sought. Recall in this connection that one of the main reasons for excluding hearsay evidence is that it denies the opposing party the opportunity to challenge its reliability through cross-examination.

The form of questions asked on cross-examination is considerably less restricted than it was on direct examination. Leading questions are readily permitted because the attorney is not trying to prompt the witness, but rather is trying to show either that the witness is mistaken about a particular fact, or perhaps that the witness is not worthy of belief because of personal shortcomings. These modes of attacking a witness on cross-examination are often referred to as "impeachment" of the witness. Although cross-examination permits considerable latitude for attacking a witness' testimony, argumentative questions are still excluded.

What were the basic points Mr. Mulvey was trying to make on cross-examination? Why did Mr. Mulvey ask about the plaintiff's tax records? What was the reason for the "Airman-of-the-Month" line of questioning? Was it successful? Can you explain the dispute over the 1941 conviction?

Redirect Examination by Mr. Lisman:

Q. When were you shipped overseas to Newfoundland, Sergeant?

A. September 6, 1958.

Q. So you were here in this country for how long after the newspaper articles appeared in St. Albans?

A. November, 1957 until then.

Q. That would be about ten months? Nine or ten months?

A. Nine or ten months. Somewhere in there.

Q. Now Mr. Mulvey made a point that it must have been necessary for you to explain to your friends the plea of guilty to the offense of driving while under suspension. Do you remember him asking you about that?

A. Yes, I do.

Q. And you told him it was necessary for you to explain it to your friends, is that right?

A. That's right.

Q. I show you Plaintiff's 1 and ask you if that is what you used in explaining to your friends about this driving under suspension?

A. That's right.

Q. And did you have any difficulty with your friends and other people about the reports of your having pleaded to driving under suspension?

A. Not after I got that.

Mr. Lisman: We offer Plaintiff's 1.

Mr. Mulvey: We object to this offer. It is self-serving. Certainly Mr. Marsh isn't here to be cross-examined. He can say how he explained to his friends if he wants to.

Mr. Lisman: I don't see how a letter from the Commissioner of Motor Vehicles can be self-serving by this man. He didn't write it.

The Court: Plaintiff's 1 may be admitted.

Mr. Mulvey: May we have an exception on the ground that this is strictly hearsay. I don't have the right to examine the sender of it. Secondly it is self-serving. Number three, it itself contains hearsay.

Mr. Lisman: If the Court please, I should like to read Plaintiff's 1 to the jury.

The Court: Why don't we turn the exhibit over to the jury and let them read it while you are continuing your examination. It may save a little time. We will be taking our recess at three o'clock. Why don't you leave the subject until then and they can have it during their recess.

Mr. Lisman: All right.

Q. Now, Mr. Mulvey also made a reference to an Air Force order concerning your serving as deputy sheriff. Do you remember that reference?

A. I do.

Q. What was that order?

A. The order was that the Air Force would rather not have us participate in the law enforcement of civilians.

Q. And after that order was issued you ceased to serve as a civilian deputy sheriff, is that right?

A. That is right.

Q. That was the order that Mr. Mulvey was talking about?

A. That's right.

Q. It wasn't any order having to do with how you had conducted yourself in your office?

A. Oh, no.

Q. This was a general order, was it?

A. To the complete Air Force, right.

Q. Will you tell us again, since the question has come up again, why you sold your house in Fairfax?

A. Why I sold my house in Fairfax?

Mr. Mulvey: Excuse me, didn't you go all through this on direct examination?

Mr. Lisman: You have raised it again on cross-examination. Now I have got to straighten it out again.

The Court: This is about the third time, but we will allow it.

A. I sold it to get away from the ridiculing around that little town.

Q. Did you sell it in order to buy another place in Enosburg?

A. No. I sold it for that one reason, and I bought one in Enosburg.

Q. You bought one in Enosburg right after you sold the one in Fairfax?

A. Right about the same time.

Mr. Mulvey: This is his witness, he doesn't have to lead. Just ask the questions.

Mr. Lisman: Yes, he is right.

Q. Was one of your purposes in selling the house in Fairfax to buy a house in Enosburg?

A. No.

Q. Now, Mr. Mulvey has also asked you how you knew that the reason people stopped doing business with you was that the St. Albans Messenger had said that you were convicted of driving drunk. Do you remember his asking you that?

A. Something like that.

Q. I show you again Plaintiff's 4 and ask you if that is one of the ways you knew?

A. That's right.

Mr. Lisman: We re-offer Plaintiff's 4.

The Court: Mr. Mulvey?

(At the bench)

Mr. Mulvey: We object to the offer of Plaintiff's 4 on the ground that it is hearsay; its very words are prejudicial; no proper foundation has been laid for it; and Mr. Mulvey on his [cross] examination asked him only how he could distinguish from the effect of the C & N death resulting charge and the driving under suspension charge and the driving while under the influence of liquor charge.

The Court: Mr. Lisman?

Mr. Lisman: Mr. Mulvey has correctly stated he asked the witness on cross-examination how he could tell whether people had stopped doing business with him because of a conviction of C & N driving, death resulting, or on account to his conviction for driving while under suspension or on account of the report he had been driving drunk. Plaintiff's 4 answers that question directly.

Mr. Mulvey: The sender of Plaintiff's 4 is not here.

Mr. Lisman: The question was how he knew; this is how he knows.

The Court: The Court will allow Plaintiff's 4, with an exception to the defendant, on the ground that the matter was opened up by questions asked by Mr. Mulvey on cross-examination.

Mr. Mulvey: You have my exceptions on the record and, further, I want to point out that the matter of cross-examination had been opened up by the plaintiff and I pursued it only as far as he did.

The Court: Plaintiff's 4 may be admitted.

Q. I show you Plaintiff's Exhibit 4 and ask you whether the last paragraph of that letter showed you why it was that people had stopped doing business with you?

A. Right.

Q. Read it to us, please, that last paragraph.

A. "You know, I would sure hate to have a beer bottle for a tube in my radio."

Q. By whom is that signed, that letter?

A. Douglas C. Decker.

Q. I think you told us before he was one of your former customers. Without burdening the record, I show you these other letters from customers, Plaintiff's 5, 6, 7 and 8, and ask you if they are all to the same effect. Are they the same sort of letters?

A. They are.

Q. Differently worded?

A. Differently worded, but all meaning the same.

Q. And after those letters arrived, did you have any more business in your television and radio shop?

A. I had it for a little while; then it died right off completely.

Q. Was it just as good after the letters arrived as it had been before?

A. No. Because I lost my best customers.

Mr. Lisman: You may inquire.

Recross Examination by Mr. Mulvey:

Q. Mr. Decker, Douglas C. Decker; you know him pretty well?

A. I do.

Q. Has he been living in Fairfax for some time?

A. I don't know how long.

Q. What does he do for a living?

A. Salesman now.

Q. He is a pretty good friend of yourself?

A. No, I just know him, that's all.

Q. Fairfax is just a small town, isn't it?

A. That's right.

Q. Not much bother for Mr. Decker to walk or drive over and pick up his radio?

A. That's right.

Q. But he didn't do that. Instead, he wrote you a letter, is that right?

A. That's right.

Q. So you could use it in this trial?

A. No, he didn't know anything about it when I got that letter.

Q. He says here, "If you would bring back my car radio"—you read it.

A. "Since reading about you in the St. Albans Messenger, I don't think you are too trustworthy a person."

Q. Let's stop right here. This was dated November 29th.

A. Right.

Q. This was after the second publication in the newspaper, right?

A. Right.

Q. He also read about this previous offense of C & N, death resulting?

A. Right.

Q. But yet you say that didn't cause him to ask for his radio back, but only the DWI charge. Where do you base that?

A. Right on this paragraph on the bottom here.

Q. You base that on, "I would sure hate to have a beer bottle for a tube in my radio."?

A. That's right.

Q. Why he wouldn't want to leave it with a person who isn't trustworthy?

A. Right.

Q. He could feel, in your opinion, he could have felt you weren't trustworthy in that you were a deputy in court charged with things you had been policing other people for, right?

A. Right.

Q. In other words, because you were an officer and here you were pleading guilty to something that was considered a crime. He was mad, possibly?

A. Possibly.

Q. So he sent you a letter stating that he didn't consider you trustworthy and wanted you to bring back his radio, said he didn't want to have a beer bottle for a tube. It is very possible that you could have got this letter regardless of whether he learned you were driving while intoxicated or driving under suspension—they are both criminal offenses— you know that, don't you?

Mr. Lisman: Just a moment. May my objection be treat- ed as timely? This question on possibility is hardly evidence. I would object to it.

The Court: We will stop the line of questioning as long as it has now been objected to.

Q. Now, Mr. Towle, when I was examining you and asked you some reasons among many why you sold your house in Fairfax and purchased one in Enosburg, you said among many reasons was the one you wanted to buy one in Enos- burg, is that right?

Mr. Lisman: This is the fifth time he gets the same story. We won't object.

The Court: All right. Re-read the question, Mrs. Alex- ander, to the witness.

(Question Read)

The Court: Is that correct?

A. If memory serves me right I think about three days before I sold it I purchased the one in Enosburg.

The Court: That answer isn't responsive to the question, Mr. Towle. I don't think the question was when did you sell it. I think there was quite a bit more to the question. Re-read the question, Mrs. Alexander.

(Question Read)

A. That's right.

The Court: And the answer is, "That's right"?

A. The answer is I sold it to get away, that is the one reason among many.

Q. Among many, was the reason you wanted to buy in Enosburg?

A. My father wanted me to have that one up there.

Q. It was your father's house you bought?

A. No.

Mr. Mulvey: That is all.

(Recess)

Re-Redirect Examination by Mr. Lisman:

Q. Sergeant, something I didn't ask you before and you reminded me of it at recess, did you ever drink intoxicating liquor?

A. I do not.

Q. Have you ever?

A. No, I never have.

Q. People in Fairfax have been aware of that?

A. They should be. I never bought anything like that over there at all.

Q. It was quite a shock to them to hear you had been driving while intoxicated?

A. Some, yes.

Mr. Mulvey: If the Court please, that is objected to and ask to have the answer stricken.

The Court: All right. The question and answer may be stricken.

Re-Recross Examination by Mr. Mulvey:

Q. Mr. Towle, just a few more questions. In connection with the case of C & N driving, death resulting, I show you a copy of a court record. Would you look it over, please, and see if it is not the record of that conviction?

A.   It is. That's right.

Mr. Mulvey: It is already marked for identification De-
                fendant's B, in connection with testimony on
                that point and in connection with the answer
                which states the substantial truth of the pub-
                lication of the 26th, I offer a certified copy
                of the record of that case.

Mr. Lisman: We object to Defendant's B, especially in
                connection with the offer as made. I don't
                see how Defendant's B proves the allegation.
                This has to do with C & N driving and the
                allegation is of drunken driving. Further,
                we don't deny this conviction so there is
                no issue on which evidence should be offered
                at this time.

Mr. Mulvey: I should like to point out that the publication
                of the 26th stated this man had been convict-
                ed, had been in court on a C & N death re-
                sulting charge and been convicted, and that
                we alleged the substantial truth of that whole
                paragraph.

Mr. Lisman: In our pleadings we don't deny the truth of
                that. We deny the truth of the allegations
                of drunken driving and another one which is
                not material to C & N driving. In court
                both on direct and cross-examination the
                plaintiff stated fully and frankly he was
                convicted of C & N death resulting. I don't
                think it is an issue. This can only prej-
                udice us with the jury, the record that is
                not in issue.

The Court: We will sustain the objection.

Mr. Mulvey: Exception?

The Court: Exception.

Mr. Lisman: I was supposed to give the jury Plaintiff's
                Exhibit 1 to read when they took their recess.
                I can pass it along to them or read it, which-
                ever the Court thinks best at this time.

The Court: You don't want them, in view of the circum-
                stances of this case at the moment, to just
                take it with them when they get the case?

Mr. Lisman: I think it would be better if they had it in
                mind now.

The Court: From the time element, I think it would be faster if you go ahead and read it.

Mr. Lisman: Plaintiff's Exhibit 1 is a letter dated December 6, 1957 and signed by H. E. Marsh, Commissioner of Motor Vehicles, addressed to Ronald W. Towle, Box 7, Fairfax, Vermont, and here is the body of the letter:

"In reference to our conversation of this morning regarding your being taken into court for operating while under suspension, owing to the situation that did exist and that you did have insurance and had an operator's license from Virginia, it appears to be more or less of a technicality and, therefore, if you will file financial responsibility insurance for the future, you then may appear and take an examination for a Vermont operator's license.

"I am enclosing the insurance card and keep in mind that the insurance will have to be purchased from a company which is licensed to do business in this State."

The Court: Do you have any more questions?

Mr. Lisman: No more questions.

The Court: That is all, you may step down.

The Court: Mr. Mulvey?

Mr. Mulvey: We have no motion, if that is what you mean. We would like to get on with our case.

The Court: The Court would like to have you.

Note on Redirect and Recross Examination

Just as the process of pleading may continue back and forth until the issues are focused, so may the examination of witnesses. Each succeeding step, however, must be limited to matters raised by the previous examination. Thus, Mr. Lisman in redirect may ask only questions raised by the cross examination and on recross examination, Mr. Mulvey may ask only about issues that were raised in redirect. In this way specific fact disputes are narrowed and testimony is sharpened.

Note especially that Mr. Lisman is now permitted to introduce in evidence Douglas Decker's letter. The letter was excluded on direct examination, but is now permitted in response to something Mr. Mulvey raised on cross examination. Then Mr.

Mulvey on recross examination tries to minimize the importance of this document.

Another point worth mentioning is Mr. Lisman's reliance on the pleadings as narrowing the issues so that evidence of the sentence imposed in 1941 is inadmissible. He fears prejudice from this evidence. Why? Why is it excluded?

Mr. Lisman has not only completed his questioning of Sgt. Towle, but has also completed his entire case. He believes he has presented enough to establish his client's right to recovery, and plans no more witnesses or documents. He has presented the defamatory items, and evidence from which the jury could find that parts of them are untrue (although strictly he did not have to do this because it is up to the defense to prove that they are true). Also, he presented evidence from which the jury could estimate Sgt. Towle's damages.

At this point it is appropriate to consider how conclusively the plaintiff must present his case in order to win. Reverting to criminal law for a moment, you are probably familiar with the requirement that the prosecution prove its case "beyond a reasonable doubt" in order to convict the defendant of a crime. This rigorous standard is premised on the view that it is better that guilty men go free than that innocent men be convicted on too little evidence. In civil cases, the consequences of losing are less severe, and the party who has the burden of proof need only present enough evidence to enable a jury to decide that he has proven his case "by a fair preponderance of the evidence." It is this lesser standard that Mr. Lisman believes he has met, and he thereupon concludes his case.

The court then turns and says "Mr. Mulvey?" Mr. Mulvey responds "We have no motion, if that is what you mean." This exchange means that if Mr. Mulvey thought that Mr. Lisman had failed to present enough evidence from which the jury could find for the plaintiff "by a fair preponderance of the evidence," Mr. Mulvey could make a "motion for a directed verdict." This motion would ask the judge to order the jury to decide the case for the defendant immediately without requiring him to call any witnesses. The judge would do this only if he thought that Mr. Lisman's case was so weak that no jury could reasonably think he had met his burden of proof. Mr. Mulvey made no such motion, presumably because he thought Mr. Lisman's case was sufficient and therefore that there was no possibility of a "directed verdict." It was then Mr. Mulvey's turn to present his case.

P. THE DEFENDANT'S CASE

Mr. Mulvey's evidence will focus on two matters. First he will try to make the jurors doubtful about matters the plaintiff must prove—especially damages. Second, he will try to prove the truth of the second story "by a fair preponderance of the evidence." Can you anticipate which witnesses Mr. Mulvey might call and what they will testify?

Dorothy E. Benton, Sworn.   Direct Examination by Mr. Mulvey:

Q.   Would you give us your name?

A.   Dorothy E. Benton.

Q.   And you are a resident of St. Albans?

A.   Yes, sir.

Q.   Who employs you?

A.   Now? Vermont Department of Social Welfare.

Q.   In 1957 who did you work for?

A.   St. Albans Daily Messenger.

Q.   And on November 25, 1957, what were your duties in connection with the St. Albans Daily Messenger?

A.   I was women's editor and I also covered some court cases, accident cases and various other duties.

Q.   I show you a paper that is marked Plaintiff's Exhibit 2 and wherein it says on the second page "Arraign Nine in Municipal Court Today", and further down there is a section that says, "Ronald Towle of Fairfax, an air policeman, formerly of Enosburg, pleaded guilty to driving while intoxicated. He paid a fine of $50 and costs of $12.30." Did you write that story?

A.   I did.

Q.   Tell us the circumstances of your acquiring that story.

A.   I took it over the phone.

Q.   From whom?

A.   The judge's secretary.

Q.   And how did you take it?

A.   I took my notes always in shorthand and with the exception of some of the charges I would abbreviate in longhand. I wrote DWI for driving while intoxicated and DWS for driving while under suspension.

Q.   In this particular case what happened?

A.   In this particular case I followed the same procedure. I wrote DWS for driving while license was suspended and I didn't make the S distinct and later when I came to transcribe my notes, I mistook it for an I, so I wrote the story "driving while intoxicated."

Q. Did you know Mr. Towle before this?

A. No, sir. Never saw him before today.

Q. At the time you wrote the story you neither knew Mr. Towle nor any of his family?

A. No.

Q. This error which you made you say was merely in transcribing your notes?

A. That's right.

Q. You continued to work for the Messenger?

A. Until October when I went to work for the Welfare Department on October 6th of last year, and I worked for the Messenger until the Friday preceding, I forget the exact date.

Q. Did Mr. Towle or anybody on his behalf inform you about this error?

A. Well, I believe someone called the Messenger and the editor brought it to my attention.

Q. How long ago was that, after the publication?

A. Two or three days probably, I don't remember exactly.

Cross Examination by Mr. Lisman:

Q. Mrs. Benton, is it?

A. Yes.

Q. You now know, of course, that the story that the sergeant here was convicted of driving while intoxicated, you know now that that was false?

A. Yes.

Q. I now show you Plaintiff's Exhibit 2, which contains the story that Mr. Mulvey quoted to you. You notice the date of the Messenger there is November 25, 1957.

A. Yes.

Q. I show you now Plaintiff's Exhibit 3 and you also note that is the Messenger dated November 26, 1957?

A. Yes.

Q. That was the next day, of course, wasn't it?

A. Umhmm.

Q. I point to a story on the front page of that paper outlined in pencil. That story also refers to Sergeant Towle, does it not?

A. Yes.

Q. Did you write that story also?

A. No, I did not.

Q. Now that story—have you read the story?

A. I have read it previously.

Q. That story was written after somebody on the Messenger discovered the error, was it not?

A. I couldn't say, I don't remember the exact date my error was brought to the attention of the Messenger. I don't think it was that soon. I think it was several days later.

Q. So you think the story in Plaintiff's Exhibit 3 was written before the Messenger discovered its error?

A. I think so.

Q. So that when the story in Exhibit 3 was written, the Messenger still thought Sergeant Towle had been convicted of driving drunk?

A. Yes.

Mr. Mulvey: I did not get that question nor the answer. I would like to hear it if I could.

Mr. Lisman: That is all.

Redirect Examination by Mr. Mulvey:

Q. Mrs. Benton, this last question was referring to the second story?

A. He asked me if I knew for sure that the—my error had been brought to the attention of the Messenger before that story was written and I said I didn't think it had.

Q. This particular story on the 26th refers to Mr. Towle pleading guilty to driving under suspension, is that right?

A. Umhmm.

Q. And that was the correct charge, is that correct?

A. That's right.

Q. So at the time of this second story—

Mr. Lisman: Just a minute. This is his witness and he cannot lead the witness.

The Court: I don't think he had finished the question.

Mr. Lisman: No, but if he finishes it, it is going to be leading.

Mr. Mulvey: In view of that I will waive the question.

The Court: All right, Mr. Mulvey.

Q. As far as you know, this story on the 26th—tell us whether or not as far as you know that was the correct charge therein stated?

A. This one? I did not write that story, you understand.

Q. I know you didn't.

A. As far as I know.

The Court: Is that all?

Mr. Mulvey: That is all, if the Court please.

Stanley R. Beauregard Sworn.   Direct Examination by Mr. Mulvey:

Q. Would you give us your name, please?

A. Stanley R. Beauregard.

Q. Where do you reside?

A. St. Albans.

Q. What is your occupation?

A. City editor of the Messenger.

Q. In 1957, specifically November 25th and 26th, were you city editor of the St. Albans Messenger?

A. Yes.

Q. I am showing you a paper marked Plaintiff's Exhibit 3 which carries a story in it that is headed "Ex-Sheriff's Patrolman Admits Count", and goes on to state that Ronald Towle was in court on the 25th and pleaded guilty to driving while under suspension and further goes on to state that he was dropped from the patrol for misuse of authority and sets forth a prior conviction of Mr. Towle for C & N, death resulting. Do you have that story in mind?

A. I do.

Q. Were you author of that story?

A. Yes.

Q. Tell us where it was written?

A. In the office of Sheriff John Finn.

Q. How was it written?

A. I don't understand the question.

Q. Typewritten or pencil?

A. Typewriter.

Q. Where did you get this information that is contained in this story?

A. From Sheriff Finn.

Q. Did you show the story to Sheriff Finn?

A. I did.

Q. Did Sheriff Finn read the story?

A. He did.

Q. Did he correct it or change it?

A. Yes.

Q. What part did he add to it, what part would you say is his authorship?

A. Two phrases.

Q. Which phrases, please?

A. One which deals with Mr. Towle being overseas and another dealing with the Air Force order against servicemen serving on civilian law enforcement.

Q. Then did the sheriff tell you that Mr. Towle had been dropped from the sheriff's patrol for misuse of authority?

A. He did.

Q. The other information contained in that article concerning previous conviction of careless and negligent driving, death resulting, were you told that by the sheriff?

A. No.

Q. Where did you get that?

A. State police.

Q. The entire article, was it read by the Sheriff?

A. Yes.

Q. Was it read before it was published?

A. Yes.

Q. Was it read as soon as you composed it?

A. Yes, it was.

Q. Did you know Mr. Towle?

A. Yes, I did.

Q. Were you with him on one occasion when a complaint was made about his actions as a deputy sheriff?

Mr. Lisman: Just a minute, I don't see how this is material.

Mr. Mulvey: Yes or no.

The Court: We will take it.

Mr. Lisman: I move to strike if it isn't connected up.

The Court: Yes.

Q. What is your answer?

A. Yes.

Q. Was that the Waterbury incident?

A. Yes.

Q. As far as the story in the paper of the 26th, is there any part of that story which you know to be untrue?

A. No.

Q. How long have you worked for the Messenger, Mr. Beauregard?

A. Completing my seventh year this month.

Q. Does any part of this story—is there any part of this story that you would want to change in light of any . . . facts any different that you know of now?

A. No.

Q. As far as you can determine, these are the facts?

A. Yes.

Q. At the time this story was published had you or had you not talked with Mr. Towle or someone in his behalf? In other words, were any complaints made to you about the previous day's story?

A. No complaints. It was called to my attention.

Q. Was this an attempt to correct the previous day's story?

A. It was.

Q. As far as you are concerned and can tell, that was true? The second story?

A. Yes.

Cross Examination by Mr. Lisman:

Q. Mr. Beauregard, have you had some training for your job? You are a journalist, are you not?

A. Yes.

Q. Have you had some training?

A. I don't understand your question.

Q. You are a high school graduate, I assume?

A. Yes.

Q. What other education have you had?

A. No formal education beyond high school.

Q. Did you take any special training for journalism?

A. No, I did not.

Q. Did you have some experience in this line before you went to work for the St. Albans Messenger?

A. Well, in high school.

Q. You worked on the high school paper?

A. I worked on the high school paper. I also worked for the Messenger while in high school.

Q. Then you went to work for the Messenger and became city editor?

A. Subsequently.

Q. Now, I show you Plaintiff's Exhibit 2. Do you recognize it as the issue of the St. Albans Daily Messenger of November 25, 1957?

A. Why, I assume it is.

Q. Did you see the story, the Messenger report, that Sergeant Towle was convicted of driving drunk?

A. I know it was in there.

Q. Do you see the story?

A. No, I don't see the story.

Mr. Mulvey: I think the record ought to show the witness has trouble in seeing.

Mr. Lisman: Yes, that is right. I am sorry.

Q. You know that story is in there?

A. Yes.

Q. Do you know now the story is false?

A. Yes.

Q. Now I show you Plaintiff's Exhibit 3. Do you recognize it as the St. Albans Messenger of the following day, November 26, 1957?

A. Yes.

Q. That is the one that contains the story that you wrote?

A. Yes.

Q. That is, the story you wrote about Sergeant Towle?

A. Yes.

Q. When you wrote that story you knew then the previous day's story was wrong, did you not?

A. I did, sir.

Q. Did you say anywhere in that second story, the story that you wrote, that Mr. Towle had not been convicted of driving while intoxicated?

A. I did not.

Q. Did you say anywhere in that story that Mr. Towle or Sergeant Towle had been the subject of a story the previous day which was not correct?

A. I did not.

Q. Did you in any way take back or retract anything of what had been written the previous day?

A. I felt it was inferred, fully covered.

Q. Did you put anything in your story to take back what had been written the previous day?

A. I felt that it was adequately covered.

Q. You felt by saying Sergeant Towle had been convicted of driving while under suspension and had been dropped from sheriff's patrol for some reasons of misconduct, that that proved to the public he was not guilty of driving while intoxicated?

A. I felt the article stated he was in court the previous day for driving under suspension and that inferred the previous day's article was incorrect.

Q. Now you have also reported that he was dropped from the patrol in June for misuse of authority. That is correct?

A. Yes, I believe it is.

Q. That was the highway patrol of Sheriff Finn you were referring to?

A. The sheriff's patrol, yes.

Q. That was the sheriff's patrol of Sheriff Finn of Franklin County?

A. Yes.

Q. Haven't you since become aware that so far as having been dropped in June he was actually working for the sheriff's patrol in July?

A. I am not aware of that.

Q. You are city editor for the St. Albans Messenger?

A. Yes.

Q. As such, facts come to your attention?

A. Yes.

Q. You still haven't learned that as late as July Sergeant Towle was still with the sheriff's patrol?

A. No, I am not aware of that.

Q. You say it was Sheriff Finn who told you he was dropped from the sheriff's patrol for misuse of authority?

A. Yes.

Q. That occurs in the newspaper in quotation marks, "misuse of authority"?

A. Yes.

Q. Was that put in quotation marks so you put this all on Sheriff Finn?

A. He was my source of information.

Q. Haven't you since learned Sergeant Towle was not suspended in June from the sheriff's patrol for misuse of authority?

A. No, I have not.

Q. Yet facts come to your attention as editor of the St. Albans Messenger, do they not?

A. Yes.

Mr. Lisman: That is all.

John R. Finn Sworn. Direct Examination by Mr. Mulvey:

Q. Would you give us your name?

A. John Roderick Finn.

Q. What is your occupation?

A. Franklin County Sheriff.

Q. Were you Franklin County Sheriff in November, 1957?

A. I was.

Q. On November 26 [sic], 1957 did you have some conversation with Stanley Beauregard regarding Sergeant Towle?

A. I did.

Q. Did this take place at the jail?

A. It did.

Q. What part of the jail?

A. In the sheriff's office.

Q. And what time of day or night?

A. Well, it was in the mid-evening on into the latter part of the night.

Q. Had it come to your attention by that time that Sergeant Towle had been in court   .   .   .?

A. I am municipal court officer so I saw him there.

Q. You were there when he pleaded guilty to driving under suspension?

A. That is correct.

Q. When Mr. Beauregard, Stanley Beauregard, wrote the story he typed it, is that correct?

A. That is right, on the jail typewriter.

Q. And he showed it to you?

A. That is correct.

Q. And you made some alterations in it, do you recall?

A. I don't remember.   I remember making alterations but I don't remember what they were.

Q. And as you saw that story and read it over, was it substantially true?

A. By and large, yes.   I would say it was true.

Q. Then you say that—had you been at that time using Sergeant Towle as a deputy?

A. No.   The last time as a matter of fact I did use Sergeant Towle was in July.   The Fourth of July there was something going on up in Franklin and he and a couple other deputies went up there.

Q. Then you say this was substantially so, you hadn't used him?

A. That is correct.

Q. Had there been occasions when there had been, as deputy sheriff, misuse of authority by him?

A. Yes, there had.

Q. Was this or was it not the reason why you were not using him?

A. This was the reason why I was not using him.   That is a fact.

Q. Now during July, between July and November, you had used other deputies, I assume?

A. That is correct; the patrol was still active.

Q. Would you call him, or what would you do?

A. I would say it was more or less an agreement between the two of us. He told me one day he had a television business— this was prior to July, I don't recall when, June maybe— and that he wouldn't be able to participate in patrol activities, so I accepted that because I didn't want to use him any more.

Q. But it is true the reason why you didn't want to use him was—

Mr. Lisman: We object. This is his witness.

The Court: I think we will let the question stand. I am not sure the frame of the question, however, is correct.

Mr. Lisman: That is what I was objecting to; it is leading.

Mr. Mulvey: I will waive it.

Q. Then the reason as stated in the paper here, on the 26th of November, and quoted, that you let him go for misuse of authority is correct, substantially?

A. Yes, if it views the whole picture. It wasn't the two letters that were shown, alone.

Q. You mean there had been other complaints?

A. The overall picture, correct. Primarily complaints from people of Fairfax.

Q. Did they complain about him as a deputy?

A. That is correct.

Q. Although you say you used other deputies for patrol, you wouldn't use him after July?

A. No, I didn't. I never called on him.

Q. Did you have the information about the insurance, failure to file insurance, at the time the story was written? Did that come up in court?

A. I am not sure what you mean. I knew of the charge, yes. I heard that on the day he was brought into court.

Q. By him?

A. No.

Q. His explanation?

A. I heard the explanation just following court, if I remember correctly.

Q. From whom?

A. From Sergeant Towle.

Q. What kind of complaints did you receive about misuse of authority from Fairfax, Mr. Sheriff, the nature of them?

A. It was a complaint by the people, some of which I disregard even today, claiming that Sergeant Towle didn't know how to use his authority as deputy sheriff, that he was belligerent, that he wasn't polite enough, and so forth and so forth. It was about the time the sheriff's patrol started and we got a lot of criticism.

Q. Did you receive complaints from Montpelier?

A. I did.

Q. From whom?

A. William Baumann, Commissioner of Public Safety.

Q. On more than one occasion?

A. I received a letter from Commissioner Baumann citing an incident which occurred in Waterbury on a day when I sent Sergeant Towle and two others to Waterbury or vicinity to pick up a prisoner, and the other one was related to me by a member of the Vermont State Police.

Q. Do you happen to have that letter with you, sir?

A. I do not.

Q. You read the story, Sheriff, as published in the newspaper on the evening of the 26th, I assume?

A. Yes, I did.

Q. You had no reason to make any complaint about the quotations in it, you didn't complain to the newspaper?

A. No, I didn't.

Mr. Mulvey: Thank you.

Cross Examination by Mr. Lisman:

Q. Should you have, Sheriff? They quoted you as using the phrase "misuse of authority." Should you have complained, Sheriff?

A. This is not an easy question to answer. So many times a sheriff or some other person in such authority is asked something, and you answer to the best of your ability.

Q. You didn't really mean to claim that Sergeant Towle was suspended in June for misuse of authority, did you?

A. It was the shortest title to a book, is all I can say.

Q. If he misused his authority, Sheriff, he would have been found guilty of violation of your organizational rules, wouldn't he?

A. Well, I did not use—well, to answer your question, that is correct.

Q. There were certain rules, not written rules, that deputy sheriffs follow?

A. Yes.

Q. Not supposed to misuse their authority, correct?

A. Yes.

Q. If they had done that they would be guilty of violation of your organizational rules, that's correct, isn't it?

A. That is correct.

Q. Sheriff, I show you a letter dated December 3, 1957. Do you recognize the signature?

A. I do.

Q. Is the whole letter in your own handwriting?

A. That is correct.

Q. Does it start off, "December 3, 1957. To Whom it May Concern—"

Mr. Mulvey: Just a moment, please, I don't think that is in evidence.

Mr. Lisman: This is being done for impeachment.

Mr. Mulvey: I still don't think it is proper.

Q. This has been identified as being under your own signature and under your own handwriting?

A. Has it? I believe so. It is my letter.

Q. Does it start off, "December 3, 1957. To Whom it May Concern: Ronald Towle was never suspended from the Franklin County Sheriff's patrol for violation of organizational rules"?

A. That is what it says.

Q. It is your handwriting?

A. That is correct.

Q. And it is signed by you?

A. That is correct.

Q. Sheriff, is there more than one newspaper in the city of St. Albans?

A. There is one newspaper published in the city of St. Albans as the St. Albans Messenger.

Q. Is there any other daily newspaper?

A. Not published in Franklin County.

Q. There is a weekly newspaper, the Swanton Courier?

A. Published in Enosburg, correct.

Q. But the only daily newspaper in Franklin County is the St. Albans Messenger, is that correct?

A. That is correct.

Q. How many times have you been elected sheriff?

A. Twice.

Q. Did you have the support of the St. Albans Messenger each time?

A. I think I had the support of the Messenger, as much as they could support any political figure.

Q. If you run for sheriff again you would like to have their support again?

A. It is always nice to have.

Mr. Lisman: Of course it is. Thank you, Sheriff.

Redirect Examination by Mr. Mulvey:

Q. You never have stated that Mr. Towle was suspended for violation of organizational rules, have you?

A. I never told as such. Never used the words, "Sergeant, you are suspended." I just stopped using him.

Q. You just suspended him yourself?

A. That is correct.

Q. And that was for abuse of authority?

A. That is correct.

Q. No particular violation of any particular rule. You don't have by-laws, do you?

A. No. More or less the laws as set forth in the Vermont statutes control us. Those are our by-laws.

Q. If a particular man doesn't meet your particular standard and you believe he is not a good officer you just don't use him, is that correct?

A. That is correct.

Q. And you concluded not to use this gentleman, Mr. Towle?

A. That is correct.

Q. That conclusion was based on what you determined was misuse of authority, correct?

Mr. Lisman: I object to that. It is leading, Your Honor.

The Court: I think in my discretion I will let that stand. You can answer this, Sheriff.

A. I felt it would be much better if Sergeant Towle were not on sheriff patrol and I, therefore, did not use him.

Q. And you read the article before it was printed, we are talking about, of November 26th?

A. Yes.

Q. As you have testified, it was substantially true?

A. Yes, as far as I could see it was, by and large so.

Recross Examination by Mr. Lisman:

Q. Sheriff, you said you read this article over before it was published?

A. That is correct.

Q. In other words, you support Mr. Beauregard in that claim.

A. I read the article over, that is correct.

Q. You corrected it? He says you did.

A. I corrected something relative to the history, I believe.

Q. You corrected whatever you noticed was wrong?

A. I can't say that. I am not now a newspaper reporter. I, therefore, don't write the reporters' story for them.

Q. There may have been things in there wrong that you didn't correct?

A. I didn't say there was anything wrong.

Q. Are you aware the story says Sergeant Towle was suspended from the patrol in June? Is that the way you remember the story?

A. I haven't seen that story for quite awhile so I don't remember what it says.

Q. It is right in the second paragraph there. Read it.

A. "Ronald Towle of Fairfax, who was dropped from the patrol in June"—that's what the story says.

Q. That isn't so, of course, is it?

A. Since that time Mr. Towle and I stood outside and set down the date of the last time, which was July 4, 1957.

Q. But it wasn't correct he was suspended or dropped in June?

A. At that time as far as I could remember it was June.

Q. At that time it was November of the same year and you can remember better in September of two years later than you could in November of the same year?

A. No, sir. The two of us talked it out there while you stood there. We set the time.

Q. You know now that June was wrong?

A. That's right.

Q. But you thought June was right at the time you saw the story?

A. At that time as far as I could remember.

Q. You realize now your memory at that time was a little faulty?

A. It is like any other human being's—faulty.

Q. You would rather take the position your memory at that time was faulty than to take the position now that the story is not correct, is that right?

A. I am not taking any position on that.

Q. You won't say one way or the other whether the story is correct?

A. The position I take—I was not using Sergeant Towle on patrol because of the complaints that I had received from the good people of the town of Fairfax and from the order of Air Force officials, I hadn't used him for several months, and that is essentially the story.

Q. But not for misuse of authority?

A. Generally, it was misuse of authority. The town people claimed misuse of authority.

Q. Do you think you are going to have the support of the St. Albans Messenger when you run again for sheriff?

A. I don't know.

Mr. Lisman: I think you will. That is all.

Re-Redirect Examination by Mr. Mulvey:

Q. It certainly wouldn't make any difference to you in your testimony here whether you had that support or not, would it?

A. I hope not sincerely.

Mr. Mulvey: That is all.

The Court: Defendant rests?

Mr. Mulvey: Defendant rests.

The Court: Any rebuttal?

Mr. Lisman: No rebuttal, Your Honor. Plaintiff rests.

The Court: The evidence is closed. (3:55 p. m.)
Ladies and Gentlemen, we will now recess until nine-thirty tomorrow morning. I think I do owe you an ex-

planation. Both parties have rested; we still have arguments of counsel, the charge of the Court and your deliberations. After our conference at the Bench it appears that the matters at least of arguments of counsel and charge of the Court would get us quite along into the evening. So we will recess now until nine-thirty tomorrow morning, but you have my promise that prior to noon tomorrow, and I hope much before noon, you will have the case. We will recess now until nine-thirty tomorrow morning.

Note After Defendant's Case

Turning first to the testimony of Dorothy Benton, what was Mr. Mulvey trying to establish? What does the testimony of Stanley Beauregard add to the defense? Finally, why did Mr. Mulvey call Sheriff Finn? What do you think of Mr. Lisman's cross-examination of the Sheriff?

At the close of the examination of Sheriff Finn, Mr. Mulvey rested his case. The court then asked Mr. Lisman whether he wished to call any witnesses in "rebuttal" of the defendant's case. Mr. Lisman's scope for rebuttal, like his "redirect" examination of one of his own witnesses, would be limited to matters already raised by his adversary. He chose to offer none and the evidence was declared closed at 3:55 p. m. that afternoon.

Q. THE CASE GOES TO THE JURY

Now that the evidence has been concluded our focus shifts to the jury, although the defendant may make one last try to keep the case from the jury by making another "motion for a directed verdict." As in the earlier directed-verdict motion, made after only the plaintiff's case, the defendant contends that the plaintiff's evidence is insufficient to present any fact issue for a jury. Neither party made any such motion in the Towle case because everyone recognized that the issues presented were so disputed that a jury had to resolve them.

The following morning, September 25, 1959, the attorneys met in Judge Hill's chambers to go over some preliminaries before submitting the case to the jury. This is the transcript of what took place at that time.

Mr. Lisman: If the Court please, at this time the plaintiff moves to strike the evidence concerning complaints made against the plaintiff by various members of the public, some of them relayed through the Commissioner of Public Safety or his department.

We objected to these pieces of evidence as they came up and they were admitted by the Court subject to counsel for the defendant tying them in, with leave to the plaintiff to move to strike if they were not so tied in. The plaintiff says that they are not tied in because no evidence was offered of the truth of these complaints. The plaintiff, therefore, moves to strike that evidence.

The Court: Mr. Mulvey?

Mr. Mulvey: There is in the case ample evidence to tie in the complaints to this plaintiff. The plaintiff himself admitted on the stand that he had knowledge himself of complaints or a complaint from the Commissioner of Public Safety Baumann when I cross-examined him regarding the letter received from Baumann. The sheriff testified he himself had received complaints as he put it, "from the good people of Fairfax", regarding Mr. Towle's activity as a deputy. And he further testified on the basis of these complaints he suspended him from the sheriff's patrol as of July 4th. The question in issue is whether or not the sheriff in fact suspended this man from the sheriff's patrol for abuse of authority, and the complaints show that the sheriff considered this action or claimed action as abuse of authority and so suspended Mr. Towle.

The Court: Motion to strike denied with exception to the plaintiff.

Mr. Mulvey: I would like to make a motion to strike from the evidence—I don't know if I properly saved my right to do so, but I want to make a motion to strike evidence as regards damages in connection with two items: the item wherein the plaintiff testified that he sold his house, valued in his opinion at about $5500, for $4500. The basis for this motion to strike is that he did not tie that up in any direct or indirect manner with the claimed libel. Second, that the fact he sold the house for a certain price does not necessarily prove he had to sell the house. We say such damages in this respect are at best speculative.

My second portion of the motion is directed to that section wherein the plaintiff claims, implies at least in evidence, he suffered because he did not receive the promotion he was "in line for". There is no evidence he did not receive a promotion because of these alleged libels. There is no evidence that he would have gotten these promotions, this promotion, except for the fact of these publications. The evidence, if it were allowed to stay in the case would be at best speculative, completely speculative. The jury would be speculating on whether or not he would have received a promotion had not these been made, without any evidence on those particular points.

Therefore, on the grounds set forth, I move those particular elements of damages be stricken and the jury be so instructed.

Mr. Lisman: This evidence was none of it objected to when it came in. Motion to strike is not the way to reach it. This is not the one. Not only that, we say the house matter was gone over five or six times, plaintiff trying to show the sale of the house was caused by this libel and defendant trying to show it wasn't. It is now an issue for the jury so far as relevance is concerned.

So far as the promotion matter is concerned, I think there is enough evidence on the record to warrant submission to the jury. It is impossible to tell what, at this time, what that evidence is. It is not identified in the record. Some of it is tied in with other evidence. It wasn't objected to. This isn't the way to reach it at all and certainly right to file a motion to strike was not reserved as the evidence came in.

Mr. Mulvey: When the evidence is coming in the defendant has no way of knowing whether or not such evidence will be connected up with the particular issue, and he can't tell until all the evidence is closed whether or not that will happen. He can't be in position continually to make objection to evidence which in itself is unobjectionable if it is going to be tied in. So the only way the defendant can bring this to the court's attention is after the close of the case. Rebuttal also.

The Court: As far as the motion to strike is concerned, in both instances it is denied.

How effective is a "motion to strike evidence" from the jury's consideration? Granting Mr. Mulvey's point that evidence is often admitted subject to later connection with the case and is then not connected, how can it be "removed" from the case? Recent empiric studies have shed some light on this problem. As you may have inferred from the Towle trial, it is impermissible for the plaintiff to tell the jury that the defendant is insured. Why? Recently, a personal injury case was tried before a series of 30 experimental juries. The facts of the accident were constant throughout. The defendant's insurance status was the sole variable. In one set of ten trials the defendant was shown to have no insurance; in a second set defendant was shown to have insurance but no further notice was given the matter; and in the third, when defendant was shown to have insurance the court explicitly told the jury to disregard that fact. Since the defendant's liability for the accident was equally clear in all cases, any variation in the damages awarded could be traced to the insurance differences. In the first set verdicts averaged $33,000. How would you expect the average verdicts to run in the other two sets?

The attorneys returned to the courtroom for their closing arguments to the jury. Each attorney has his opportunity to restate the evidence coherently and to urge upon the jurors those inferences and conclusions favorable to his client that could be drawn from this evidence. For example, Mr. Lisman might emphasize the sheriff's letter and also urge the jurors to conclude that Sgt. Towle's overriding reason for selling his Fairfax property was the libel. Mr. Mulvey might argue that there was little or no difference between the actual and the falsely charged crimes, pointing out that a first offender guilty of driving while under the influence of intoxicating liquor shall be fined not less than $50 nor more than $500, or imprisoned up to two years, or both. The penalty for driving with a suspended license is a fine of not more than $500 or imprisonment up to two years, or both. Is this argument persuasive?

Unfortunately, the closing arguments were not transcribed so we can only speculate about what was said. We know that Mr. Lisman as plaintiff's attorney was entitled to make the final closing argument. We also know that Mr. Mulvey spent approximately an hour in his closing argument and that Mr. Lisman spent some 20 minutes. Despite the freedom of scope for argument attorneys may not go beyond, nor distort, the evidence. Nor, of course, may the attorney appeal to racial, religious or regional bias. Although the arguments were not transcribed, the following exchange during Mr. Mulvey's closing argument was reported:

Mr. Lisman: May the record show that counsel is arguing that the fact that one crime was charged when another was admitted did not necessarily result in any damage. We say that is not the law and counsel should not be allowed to argue that.

The Court: We think you are getting into the province of the Court, Mr. Mulvey and the Court will ask the jury to disregard that last statement as being a statement of law by counsel.

Mr. Mulvey: If the Court please, I would certainly like an exception to that. I am merely stating my position in the case, I am stating what our position has been.

I will reword that remark, if I have the Court's permission, to say the fact a person is accused of one crime and the newspaper prints another crime, certainly ought to be taken in consideration when you arrive at the question of damage.

―――――

Another interesting point in Mr. Lisman's closing argument was that although at the earlier meeting in chambers he had asserted that the jury had enough evidence from which it could reasonably find a causal relation between the newspaper's defamation and Sgt. Towle's loss of promotion, he must have had second thoughts because during his closing argument he apparently told the jury that the claim of loss of promotion was being withdrawn from the case. Mr. Lisman may have been worried about insufficient evidence and feared that if this claim remained a new trial might be necessary.

After the closing arguments, the judge will "charge" the jury by telling them the appropriate legal rules to use in reaching a result. He compiles this charge partly from his own research and also from requests delivered to him in writing by each attorney. The following request from Mr. Mulvey is a good example.

———

Ronald Towle
    vs
St. Albans Publishing
Company, Inc.
                     Chittenden County Court

REQUEST TO CHARGE

The defendant respectfully requests the Court to charge as follows:

1. Truth is an absolute defense to an action of libel. In this case we are concerned with two publications. The first was on November 25, 1957 where the paper published that Mr. Towle, the plaintiff, had pleaded guilty to Driving While Under the Influence of Intoxicating Liquor. It is admitted by all that he had in fact pleaded guilty to driving a motor vehicle while his license so to do had been suspended by the Commissioner of Motor Vehicles. The defendant states that the error was an inadvertent one and that the crime that the plaintiff had in fact committed is of the same gravity as that published, and thus no damages would flow from such a publication and I so charge.

2. The second publication occurred on November 26, 1957. This was the story regarding Mr. Towle being dropped from the Sheriff's patrol. The defendant claims that this story is true. If you find that this story is true in every substantial part then you cannot award any damages for that publication.

3. If you do come to the element of damages you will award only such damages as naturally flowed from the alleged libels and is in evidence and if you find that no damages flowed from the alleged libels then you will return a verdict for the defendant.

Respectfully submitted,

/s/ John Mulvey
Attorney for the Defendant

The judge will read his synthesis of the charges requested and his own research to the jurors. Imagine yourself in the position of a juror and read the following instructions by Judge Hill slowly and once only; in most states you will not be given a copy of the judge's charge to take to the jury room. If the jurors disagree about what the judge said (or about some testimony) they will come back and ask to have the disputed portion reread by the court stenographer.

If an attorney disagrees with the judge's charge, he must object to the specific passage when the judge concludes. He will be barred from raising any point to which he did not object unless the judge's mistake was a serious basic error such as failure to mention the issue of truth.

COURT'S CHARGE TO THE JURY

Ladies and Gentlemen, we will appoint Mr. Johnson as your foreman.

This matter is an action of libel brought by Mr. Towle against the St. Albans Publishing Company which publishes the St. Albans Daily Messenger, wherein Mr. Towle alleges that on the 25th day of November, 1957 the St. Albans Messenger published a news item to the effect that he, Mr. Towle, had pleaded guilty to driving while intoxicated. As to that allegation by Mr. Towle, because of the falsity of that allegation, which has been admitted by the defendant, the Court charges you that as to that allegation we have what is known as a libel per se, and the defendant as to that allegation is guilty of the libel, and I so charge you.

The plaintiff further says that on the 26th day of November, 1957, the defendant, through its newspaper the St. Albans Daily Messenger, published a second article and in the second article falsely stated that the plaintiff Mr. Towle was dropped from the sheriff's patrol for misuse of authority. As to this second allegation, the Court will charge you that the defense to the allegation alleged by the defendant is that such allegation was true, that in fact Mr. Towle was dropped from the sheriff's patrol for misuse of authority, and the Court charges you that if you find from all of the evidence that such statement was true, then the defendant as to this aspect of the case should be relieved of any responsibility.

Now the burden, as we say, is upon the plaintiff to make out and establish every essential element of his case, that is, to prove his case by a fair balance of the evidence, or, as it is sometimes called, by a preponderance of the evidence. You will understand this expression better if you conceive that you are weighing the evidence of the respective parties as in a balance, that of the plaintiff on one side and that of the defendant on the other. If the plaintiff's evidence makes down weight, he is entitled to your verdict; if the defendant's evidence makes down weight or if the scales hang even, then your verdict should be for the defendant.

Preponderance of the evidence does not consist merely in having a greater number of witnesses than the opposing party, for as has been said, witnesses are to be weighed and not counted, although if all the witnesses are of equal credit, the number on one side or on the other may be taken into account. However, in the last analysis, it is a question of credibility, and of this you are the sole judges.

The credibility of the witnesses and the weight to be given to their testimony are questions entirely for your determination. The law is that you are not bound to give the same weight to the testimony of each witness but you should give their testimony such weight as you think it is fairly entitled to receive after considering their appearance on the stand; their candor or lack of candor; their feelings or bias, if any; their interest in the result of the trial, if any; their opportunities for observation; their means of information, and the reasonableness of the testimony which they give. In other words do their stories have such a true ring, bear such a stamp of credit, that you consider them believable and safe to rely upon as a guide to the truth? Is it probable in the natural course of events that the witnesses could and would have heard and seen correctly, remembered accurately and testified here truthfully about the things they say they heard and saw? It is all a question for your sound, practical judgment as fair-minded men and women.

It is your duty to reconcile conflicting testimony if you can upon the theory that all of the witnesses have sworn to the truth, but if you cannot do so, then you are to determine from all the evidence before you which of the witnesses is entitled to the greater credit. Oftentimes, two or more persons, witnesses of a certain occurrence, differ in their narratives of what occurred, and that difference is not the result of any untruthfulness but from the fact they either saw it or heard it from a different standpoint or else they remembered it differently. In fact, because of human limitations this is often the situation where there are numerous details to be observed. The average person cannot observe or remember each detail in such a situation accurately. Now there may have been some inconsistent statements which have appeared in this case, and there again it is your duty as fair-minded men and women to determine which of any inconsistent statements you are to believe.

Any testimony which the Court has stricken from the record is to be disregarded by you and not taken into your deliberations in any fashion. There has been certain testimony stricken and I charge you that that testimony is to be disregarded.

There are certain exhibits which have been admitted in the case. These exhibits will be taken by you into the jury room and you may give as much weight to these exhibits as you, as fair-minded men and women, feel they deserve.

As has been stated many times before, the law of the case is not what counsel may have indicated in argument nor what you feel it might be, but the law is that which the Court gives to you in the particular case, and in this matter I charge you that as to the first publication, it constitutes libel; it was admittedly false, and for that libel the plaintiff is entitled to damages. As to the second publication, which the defendant alleged as the truth, your problem is, is that second publication true. If it is, you can then disregard the second publication.

Now in the matter of libel as to the first publication, as the Court has charged, you have the problem of damages, certainly, as to the first publication. Your damages can be, first, nominal damages, which are the result of a legal right being invaded, and the plaintiff must recover some damages, called nominal, even though you find no evidence of actual damage. Nominal damages are damages so small in amount as to show they are not intended to be the actual damages to the plaintiff. If however, in your discussions you go to the problem of damages, you may consider the following:

The plaintiff has alleged that by reason of this libel published by the St. Albans Publishing Company, he has lost his good name and reputation for integrity among his neighbors and associates; that his neighbors and friends have refused to have any transactions, acquaintance and discourse with him; and that he thereby has been caused such trouble and has been brought into public scandal, infamy and disgrace. He has also stated he lost some or all of his television business, that he has been forced to sell his house and has submitted evidence as to possible value thereof. As counsel have stated, the matter of a promotion is to be disregarded by you and you will not consider in this case any possible loss that might have occurred through the promotion or loss of promotion, because insufficient evidence was given to you to show any possibility of such loss, and the Court charges you that you will not take into consideration such a possible loss.

There is no right which persons regard as more sacred than that of a good name and reputation and nothing in relation to which they are more sensitive than to an imputation upon their character. Pain, distress and anxiety of mind is the usual and necessary consequence of such a libelous imputation. The ignominy caused by the sudden loss of good reputation in the community, if you so find it, is an important element in estimation of damages in actions of this character.

You will, therefore, allow such sum as you consider just and reasonable to compensate the plaintiff for such injuries of this nature as you may find to be the direct and natural consequence of the defamatory words spoken. And as to this, you will consider what has appeared here in evidence—what was the plaintiff's reputation and standing before the words were published, how far he has fallen in the good opinion of his friends and neighbors and has been denied their association, what if any rumors were current as a result of the words printed, what has appeared here as to his sufferings in his mind. And when you have considered all those things, then you will say what sum of money will be a just and proper compensation for his injuries.

The damages that I have mentioned to you are known as compensatory damages, that is, they are to be awarded as compensation or payment for the actual injuries suffered. But in this case, if you find for the plaintiff as we have charged you as to the first of the offenses, you may award, in addition to compensatory damages, what are known as exemplary or punitive damages. Exemplary damages are not recoverable as a matter of legal right; such damages always depend on the particular case and what you find as to the circumstances. Such damages are regarded as punishment, as stamping the acts of the defendant with the jury's condemnation or disapproval, not as compensation. And in awarding them, you are to be governed wholly by the malice or wantonness of the defendant as shown by the conduct for which you find him liable. Malice in its common acceptation means ill will against a person but in its legal sense it means a wrongful act done intentionally without just cause or excuse. And so in this case you may award punitive damages if you find the defendant's acts were deliberate, intentional and persistent.

The issue here again is, first, as to the publication of November 25th, this was libelous and you are to find damages in accordance with the law of damages as the Court has given it to you. As to the publication of the 26th, the issue is, were they true. If they are true, then you will disregard them. If they were not true, you will consider them as to damages in the same light that I have charged you on damages as to the first allegation.

A lawsuit is not a battle to be won by appeal to sympathy or prejudice. It is a serious proceeding to the end that justice may be done—a way of discovering the right. A celebrated Englishman, Lord Morley, said once, "Right and wrong are in the nature of things. They are not words and phrases, they are in the nature of things." So, Ladies and Gentlemen, it is your inquiry into the nature of the things which have appeared here in evidence that will, I am confident, enable you to discern the right of this matter and bring in a true and just verdict.

I want to again suggest to you that the finding of facts in this case is entirely for you. The law is for the Court, and whatever reference the Court has made to the evidence or the claims of the parties is only for the purpose of making application of the principles of law to the issues in this case and without any purpose of indicating in the least degree how the Court may think that the case ought to be decided on the facts. That is for you to determine.

Your verdict will be in writing. You will be given a blank plaintiff's verdict and a blank defendant's verdict. If your verdict is for the plaintiff, and certainly in this instance there must be a verdict for the plaintiff on the first charge, the foreman will insert in the blank space the amount of damages you find and your foreman will sign that verdict and return it. If your verdict is for the defendant, your foreman will simply sign that verdict and return it into court. But I charge you again, there must be a plaintiff's verdict in this matter for at least nominal damages.

The Court: Do you gentlemen have any suggestions?

Mr. Mulvey: I want to except to the Court's failure to charge as requested in paragraph I of its request to charge, which in substance is if the jury find the crime published and the crime the plaintiff had in fact committed had the same gravity or criminality and the publication of this crime led to the damages, then they should award no damages for the plaintiff.

I would also except to that portion of the Court's charge wherein he said that if they find that the publication of the 26th were true, then the newspaper would have no responsibility. It is my contention that this charge did not go far enough and the jury should be instructed that if they find that this story of the 26th is true, then they should not award any damages on account of this particular story.

Further, the Court should make a charge as regards mitigation of damages and tell the jury in substance that if the publication was an inadvertent mistake or if there were no malice, then they should consider that item in mitigating any damage.

The Court: Now, Ladies and Gentlemen of the Jury, the Court is going to charge you on a supplementary matter which I failed to bring out in my first charge. Restating the issues, the Court charges you that the publication of November 25th was libelous and for that the plaintiff is entitled to damages as charged by the Court.

Secondly, that as to the publication of November 26th, the defendant has alleged the truth of the statements, and if you find that the publication of the 26th was true, then you are to award no damages for that publication. If, however, you find that the allegation of misuse of authority was not true, then you will award damages on the same basis that the Court has charged you earlier.

Further, as a general rule, mitigating circumstances in the law of defamation can be taken into account by you. These mitigating circumstances are those which, while not proving the truth of the publication tend to some appreciable degree toward such proof, and thus permit of an inference that the defendant was not actuated by malice.

(At the Bench)

Mr. Mulvey: The defendant excepts to the Court's failure to charge that the mistake of the defendant, if proved by the defendant, is to be considered as a mitigating circumstance in regard to any award of damages.

The Court: I turn the jury over to you, Mr. Officer. (11:10 a. m.)

Do you feel that, as a juror, you now have sufficient grasp of the rules to discuss a verdict? Note that this charge directs the jury to award the plaintiff at least "nominal damages" because of the first story's falsity. Notice how much is implied by this direction. The judge has decided from his study of the Vermont law the following propositions: (1) that the first story must be read as an adverse reflection on plaintiff's reputation and is therefore defamatory; (2) that defendant's failure to attempt to prove it to be true conclusively establishes its falsity; (3) that defendant's showing of inadvertent mistake is irrelevant on this issue; (4) that plaintiff's guilt on a different criminal charge does not alter the foregoing considerations; and (5) that every plaintiff who is falsely defamed must be awarded at least nominal damages. It is not essential that the jurors understand each step in the reasoning; it is enough that they understand the ultimate rule and its application to the case. Virtually every rule given to the jury is a similar reflection of several underlying legal propositions.

The jurors must accept the judge's rules of law, resolve a series of fact disputes and then apply the legal rules to the facts they find. How does the judge know that the jury is following his instructions? What does the jury report back to the judge? The last paragraph of the main portion of the charge indicates that the verdict is to be written on a form with blanks for a plaintiff's verdict and for a defendant's verdict, though the judge reminds the jury again that they *must* use the plaintiff's verdict form and award him at least nominal damages. Those forms state that "the defendant is (or is not) liable in manner and form as the plaintiff has alleged in his complaint" and specifies the amount of damages, if any.

This format is known as a "general verdict." The jury is asked to do all of the things the judge told them and to report only their conclusion. An alternative form, the "special verdict," is occasionally used. Here the jury would be asked a series of specific questions: Do you find the second story to be true? If not, how much damage did plaintiff suffer from this story? Do you find that he sold his house because of these libels? How much money did he lose on the sale of his house? An elaborate sequence of questions permits the judge to follow precisely the jury's conclusions. The pros and cons of the general verdict and the merits of the jury system generally are discussed in the following excerpts.

COURTS ON TRIAL

By Jerome Frank

110–111, 116–20, 126–30, 132–33, 135–37, 140–42 (1949).

I have said that, supposedly, the task of our courts is this: To make reasoned applications of legal rules to the carefully ascertained facts of particular law-suits. You will recall my crude schematization of the alleged nature of the process— R x F= D—*i. e.*, the Rules times the Facts equals the Decision. Where, in that scheme, does the jury fit in?

. . .

There are three theories of the jury's function:

(1) The naive theory is that the jury merely finds the facts; that it must not, and does not, concern itself with the legal rules, but faithfully accepts the rules as stated to them by the trial judge.

(2) A more sophisticated theory has it that the jury not only finds the facts but, in its deliberation in the jury-room, uses legal reasoning to apply to those facts the legal rules it learned from the judge. A much respected judge said in 1944 that a jury's verdict should be regarded as "the reasoned and logical result of the concrete application of the law (*i. e.*, the rules) to the facts."

On the basis of this sophisticated theory, the jury system has been criticized. It is said that juries often do not find the facts in accordance with the evidence, but distort—or "fudge"—the facts, and find them in such a manner that (by applying the legal rules laid down by the judge to the facts thus deliberately misfound) the jury is able to produce the result which it desires, in favor of one party or the other. "The facts," we are told, "are found in order to reach the result."

. . .

(3) We come now to a third theory which may be called the "realistic" theory. It is based on what anyone can discover by questioning the average person who has served as a juror— namely that often the jury are neither able to, nor do they attempt to apply the instructions of the court. The jury are more brutally direct. They determine that they want Jones to collect $5,000 from the railroad company, or that they don't want pretty Nellie Brown to go to jail for killing her husband; and they bring in their general verdict accordingly. Often, to all practical intents and purposes, the judge's statement of the legal rules might just as well never have been expressed. . . .

. . .

Are jurors to blame when they decide cases in the ways I've described? I think not. In the first place, often they cannot understand what the judge tells them about legal rules. To comprehend the meaning of many a legal rule requires special training. It is inconceivable that a body of twelve ordinary men, casually gathered together for a few days, could, merely from listening to the instructions of the judge, gain the knowledge necessary to grasp the true import of the judge's words. For these words have often acquired their meaning as the result of hundreds of years of professional disputation in the courts. The jurors usually are as unlikely to get the meaning of those words as if they were spoken in Chinese, Sanskrit, or Choctaw. . . .

Under our system, however, the courts are obligated to make the unrealistic assumption that the often incomprehensible words, uttered in the physical presence of the jurors, have some real effect on their thought processes. . . . Decisions, in cases which have taken weeks to try, are reversed on appeal because a phrase, or a sentence, meaningless to the jury, has been included in or omitted from the charge.

. . .

Many of the precise legal rules on which, according to the conventional theory, men in their daily affairs have a right to and supposedly do rely, are found solely in upper-court opinions admonishing trial judges to use, in charges to juries, words and phrases stating those rules. But if jurors do not understand those words and phrases, and consequently do not apply those rules, then reliance on the rules is unreliable: Men who act in reliance on that purported right to rely are deceived.

. . .

At a trial, the jurors hear the evidence in a public place, under conditions of a kind to which they are unaccustomed: No juror is able to withdraw to his own room, or office, for private individual reflection. And, at the close of the trial, the jurors are pressed for time in reaching their joint decision. Even twelve experienced judges, deliberating together, would probably not function well under the conditions we impose on the twelve inexperienced laymen.

. . .

Let us, now, consider the arguments of those who defend the jury system.

(1) *Juries said to be better at fact-finding than judges.*

The first defense is that juries are better fact-finders than judges. Judge Cooley said: "The law has established this tribunal because it is believed that, from its numbers, the mode of their selection and the fact that the jurors come from all classes of society, they are better calculated to judge the motives," and "weigh the possibilities. . . than a single man, however, . . . wise . . . he may be."

Is that a correct appraisal? Would any sensible business organization reach a decision, as to the competence and honesty of a prospective executive, by seeking, on that question of fact, the judgment of twelve men or women gathered together at random—and after first weeding out all those men or women who might have any special qualifications for answering the questions? Would an historian thus decide a question of fact?

. . .

(2) *Jurors as legislators.*

I now come to the argument for the jury system most frequently advanced. It is contended that the legal rules (made by the legislatures or formulated by the judges) often work injustice, and that juries, though their general verdicts, wisely nullify those rules. This argument, strangely enough, is put forward by many of the same lawyers who insist that substantial adherence by the judges to those rules constitutes an essential of a sound civilization, since, they say, without such adherence men could not know their legal rights or intelligently handle their affairs.

. . .

In 1929, Wigmore wrote: "Law and Justice are from time to time inevitably in conflict. That is because law is a general rule (even the stated exceptions to the rules are general exceptions); while justice is the fairness of this precise case under *all* its circumstances. And as a rule of law only takes account of broadly typical conditions, and is aimed at average results, law and justice every so often do not coincide. Everyone knows this, and can supply instances. But the trouble is that Law cannot concede it: Law—the rule—must be enforced—the exact terms of the rule, justice or no justice. . . . We want justice, and we think we are going to get it through 'the law,' and when we do not, we blame 'the law.' Now this is where the jury comes in. The jury, in the privacy of its retirement, adjusts the general rule of law to the justice of the particular case. Thus the odium of inflexible rules of law is avoided, and popular satisfaction is preserved. . . ."

. . .

Does such a defense of the jury make sense? If it does, then we should reverse the theoretical roles of trial judge and jury: As obviously the judge is usually better trained at fact-finding, let him find the facts—and then let the jury decide what legal rules should be applied to those facts. Moreover, in that event, an upper court should never reverse a decision—as often such a court now does—on account of an erroneous statement, in the trial judge's instructions, concerning the proper legal rule.

The stock example cited by those who defend the jury as legal-rule defier is the refusal of many juries to apply the harsh fellow-servant rule, a legal rule which 19th century judges had made. Yet it is highly probable that the judges themselves, before long, would have abolished that judge-made rule had they not felt that the juries would not heed it in their verdicts. Subsequently, by enacted statutes, the legislatures wiped out that harsh rule. But meanwhile some juries, feeling obligated to do so, applied it with resultant injustice in those cases. It may well be, then, that judicial reliance on juries helped to perpetuate an unjust rule, to delay its eradication either by judges or legislatures. It should be noted that in the types of cases where juries do not sit—in equity suits, for instance—the judges have been less reluctant to contrive flexible rules and to revise undesirable ones. Moreover, legislatures are more prompt today in changing legal rules than they were in the days of the fellow-servant rule.

The argument that juries make better rules than judges do has at least the virtue of honestly admitting the realities—of conceding that jurors often disregard what the trial judge tells the jurors about the *R*'s. But as a rational defense of the jury system, it is surely curious. It asserts that, desirably, each jury is a twelve-man ephemeral legislature, not elected by the voters, but empowered to destroy what the elected legislators have enacted or authorized. Each jury is thus a legislative assembly, legislating independently of all others. For even if a jury does no more than nullify a legal rule by refusing to apply it in a particular law-suit, yet it is legislating, since the power to destroy legal rules is legislative power. This argument for the jury should lead to a revised description of our legislative system to show that it consists, in the case of our federal government for instance, of (1) a Senate, (2) a House of Representatives, and (3) a multitude of juries.

I have one objection to such a description: I think it too sophisticated. It implies that the members of the ordinary jury say to themselves, "We don't like this legal rule of which the judge told us, and we won't apply it but will apply one of our own making." But when, as often happens, juries do not understand what the judge said to them about the applicable rule, it simply is not true that they refuse to follow it because they dislike it. Many juries in reaching their verdicts act on their emotional responses to the lawyers and witnesses; they like or dislike, not any legal rule, but they do like an artful lawyer for the plaintiff, the poor widow, the brunette with the soulful eyes, and they do dislike the big corporation, the Italian with a thick, foreign accent. We do not have uniform jury-nullification of harsh rules; we have juries avoiding—often in ignorance that they are so doing—excellent as well as bad rules, and in capricious fashion.

Courts frequently say that juries are especially equipped to know the "average conscience" or the "social sense of what is right" at a particular time. But can we be sure that any basis in fact exists for the supposition that any single jury does reflect the "average" views of the community? One jury may have one view, and another, summoned the next week, may have another.

. . .

The jury system, praised because, in its origins, it was apparently a bulwark against an arbitrary tyrannical executive, is today the quintessence of governmental arbitrariness. The jury system almost completely wipes out the principle of "equality before the law" which the "supremacy of law" and the "reign of law" symbolize—and does so, too, at the expense of justice, which requires fairness and competence in finding the facts in specific cases. If anywhere we have a "government of men," in the worst sense of the phrase, it is in the operations of the jury system.

. . .

If any legal rules are so inflexible that they work injustice, they should avowedly be made more flexible. The disinclination to achieve "individualization" openly, through greater flexibility in most of the R's stems from the fatuous desire to have the results of the judicial process seem more certain, more knowable, than they actually are or can be. Two desires here conflict: (1) the desire to attain certainty and uniformity, and (2) the desire to make allowance for the unique aspects of cases. We satisfy the first, verbally, by so wording many of our R's that they *seem* to exclude all discretion which would permit consideration of such uniquenesses; we then actually satisfy the second, circumventing those R's through jury verdicts by means of which such discretion runs riot. Surely, it is socially undesirable, not only to create a false appearance of legal certainty —to hide from our citizens the actual workings of our legal system—but to do so by employing so capricious an agency as the jury.

. . .

(3) *The jury as an escape from corrupt or incompetent trial judges.*

A third defense of the jury is seldom published: In a local community where some trial judges are corrupt, or subject to dictation by political bosses, or where some judges are rigid bigots or otherwise incompetent, lawyers prefer to take their chances with juries.

No one can deny that there is some force to that argument. It points to a fact I shall discuss later—that the electorate pays too little attention to the immense significance of trial courts. But unless honest, competent trial judges can be and are procured, the resort to juries is a feeble device. For, remember that, in many types of law-suits, the litigant cannot have a jury trial, must try his case before a judge without a jury.

(4) *The jury as alleged educator and creator of confidence in government.*

Another argument for the jury system is that it helps to educate citizens in government, gives them added confidence in democracy. Can that contention be proved? Do not many jurors become cynical about the court-house aspects of government? And should education in government be obtained at the expense of litigants?

(5) *Citizens said to demand this participation in government.*

Closely related to the previous argument is the contention that citizens demand participation in government through acting on juries. One wonders. If so, why do so many citizens seek to be excused from jury service?

Nevertheless, the need for popular participation in the administration of justice is the argument most frequently advanced in defense of the jury system. If we take that argument seriously—as something more than a rationalization of an irrational adherence to tradition—then we face a clash of social policies: (1) the policy favoring such popular participation undermines (2) the policy of obtaining that adequate fact-finding which is indispensable to the doing of justice. Which policy should yield? Is it less important to do justice to litigants than to have citizens serve on juries?

. . .

(8) *"Passing the Buck" to juries.*

Juries, it is argued, provide buffers to judges against popular indignation aroused by unpopular decisions. That is, the jury is an insulator for the judge, a buck-passing device. As a rational argument for the jury this seems indeed questionable.

Men fit to be trial judges should be able and willing to accept public criticism. Moreover, they are obliged to do so in the many cases they must try without juries. Probably this argument is but an ingenious rationalization.

. . .

It is extremely doubtful whether, if we did not now have the jury system, we could today be persuaded to adopt it. The chances are that most conservative lawyers would oppose such a "reform"; they would refer us to Scotland, an "Anglo-Saxon" country, where the jury has never played an important role. They would call attention to the marked decline of the jury's popularity in England. They would denounce trial by jury as an absurd New Dealish idea.

The point is that the jury, once popular thanks to its efficacy as a protection against oppression, has become embedded in our customs, our traditions. And matters traditional are likely to be regarded as inherently right. Men invoke all sorts of rationalizations to justify their accustomed ways. . . .

. . .

Nevertheless, we are saddled with the jury. For our federal and state constitutions require trial by jury in most criminal and many kinds of civil cases. In most jurisdictions, the defendant in a criminal action may waive a jury and go to trial by judge alone; both parties in a civil suit may give such waivers. The number of jury-waived cases seems to be on the increase, but the number of jury cases still remains very considerable. As it will almost surely be impossible, in the reasonably near future, to repeal the constitutional provisions concerning the jury, we must, then, face the fact that, for many years to come, the jury will be with us. Accordingly, to meet the difficulties caused by the jury system, we can today look only to palliating reforms which aim at making jurors somewhat better fact-finders. Let us now consider some proposed reforms.

1. Special (or Fact) Verdicts

. . .

A special verdict would seem to do away with some of the most objectionable features of trial by jury. The division of functions between jury and judge is apparently assured, the one attending to the facts alone, the other to the legal rules alone. The jury seems, by this device, to be shorn of its power to ignore the rules or to make rules to suit itself. . . .

. . .

It is suggested, too, that a special verdict "searches the conscience of the individual juror, as a general verdict does not," because "such are the contradictions in human nature that many a man who will unite in a general verdict for a large and unwarranted sum of money will shrink from a specific finding against his judgment of right and wrong."

[Judge Frank then discusses several other methods of "improving" jury trials, including special juries and recording jury deliberations to aid in ascertaining the existence of misconduct.]

THE DIGNITY OF THE CIVIL JURY

Harry Kalven, Jr.

50 Virginia Law Review, 1055, 1062–68, 1071–75 (1964).

As we come to the merits of the institution, it may be useful to sketch three main heads under which criticism and defense of the jury have fallen.

.   .   .

The second cluster of issues goes to the competence of the jury. Can it follow and remember the presentation of the facts and weigh the conflicting evidence? Can it follow and remember the law? Can it deliberate effectively?

The third cluster of issues goes to the adherence of the jury to the law, to what its admirers call its sense of equity and what its detractors view as its taste for anarchy.

The latter two issues go to the heart of the debate and have long been the occasion for a heated exchange of proverbs. Further, they may seem so heavily enmeshed in difficult value judgments as to make further discussion unpromising. Yet it is precisely here that our empirical studies can offer some insight, although they too cannot dispose fully of the issues.

When one asserts that jury adjudication is of low quality, he must be asserting that jury decisions vary in some significant degree from those a judge would have made in the same cases. If he denies this and wishes to include the judge, he has lost any baseline, and with it any force, for his criticism. While it is possible to say that even those juries whose decision patterns coincide with those of judges are nevertheless given to caprice, lack of understanding, and sheer anarchic disobedience to law, it is not likely that the critic means to go this far. If he does, he may have an interesting point to make about the legal order as a whole, but he has lost any distinctive point about the jury as a mode of trial. Further, trial by judge is the relevant and obvious alternative to trial by jury. To argue against jury trial is, therefore, to argue for bench trial.

Can one say anything, then, about how often judge and jury decisions agree and how often they differ? We can. One of our major research ventures has been a massive survey of trial judges on a nationwide basis. With their cooperation we were able to obtain reports on actual cases tried to a jury before them, to get the jury's verdict in each case, and to get from the judge a statement of how he would have decided the case had it been tried to him alone. Finally, the trial judge gave us his explanation of any instance of disagreement. We have, in this fashion, collected from some 600 judges, reports on some 8,000 jury trials throughout the United States for each of which we have an actual jury verdict and a hypothetical verdict from the bench. We are just completing a full, book-length, analysis of the picture thus obtained for criminal cases and plan in the ensuing year to complete the companion book reporting on the civil cases. . . .

While there are rich nuances in the patterns of jury disagreement that cannot be detailed here, we can report the main findings and place the jury system against the baseline of the bench trial system, thus giving an empirical measure of the quality of the jury performance. We shall do so first for criminal cases and then for civil cases; the contrast may help to put the performance of the civil jury in perspective.

It is evident that the matching of verdicts in criminal cases yields four possible combinations: cases where judge and jury agree to convict, where they agree to acquit, where the judge would acquit and the jury convict, and where the jury would acquit and the judge convict. Hence, the quantitative results can be readily summarized in a fourfold table. Table 1 gives the data on criminal cases.

TABLE 1

Judge and Jury Agreement and Disagreement
on Guilt in Criminal Cases

Judge Would Have Found:	Jury Found: For Defendant	Against Defendant	Total Judge
For Defendant	13	2	15
Against Defendant	18	67	85
Total Jury	31	69	100

The table contains two main conclusions. First, the jury and judge agree in the large majority of cases; to be exact in 13 per cent plus 67 per cent or 80 per cent in all. Second, the remaining 20 per cent of the cases, in which they disagree, the disagreement is generally due to the jury's being more lenient toward the criminal defendant. In summary, the overall performance of the jury is such as to produce a high degree of conformity to that of the judge, but with elbow room left for the jury to perform a distinctive function. Or, as we have put it on other occasions, the jury agrees with the judge often enough to be reassuring, yet disagrees often enough to keep it interesting.

Table 2 gives the companion figures for personal injury cases.

TABLE 2

Judge and Jury Agreement on Liability in Personal Injury Cases

Judge Would Have Found:	Jury Found:		
	For Plaintiff	For Defendant	Total Judge
For Plaintiff	44	10	54
For Defendant	11	35	46
Total Jury	55	45	100

Again we see that there is massive agreement; in the personal injury cases it runs 44 per cent plus 35 per cent or 79 per cent, almost exactly the same as for the criminal cases. Here, however, the pattern of disagreement is much more evenly balanced. The judge disagrees with the jury because he is more pro-plaintiff about as often as the jury disagrees with him because it is more pro-plaintiff. Whereas the greater leniency of the jury toward the criminal defendant is congruent with popular expectations, the equality of pro-plaintiff response between judge and jury in civil cases is in sharp contrast to popular expectations.

It must be added that Table 2 does not present quite the whole picture. If we look for the moment simply at the 44 per cent of the cases where both decide for the plaintiff, we find considerable disagreement on the level of damages. In roughly 23 per cent the jury gives the higher award, in 17 per cent the judge gives the higher award and in the remaining 4 per cent they are in approximate agreement. More important, however, is the fact that the jury awards average 20 per cent higher than those of the judge.

The two tables considered together imply that the jury's disagreement with the judge is not a random matter; they indicate something more interesting about the nature both of judge and jury as decision makers. The precise quality of that something cannot be properly sketched here. We have had considerable success in finding explanations for the instances of disagreement and thus in reconstructing a full and rounded rationale. Our thesis is that it is the jury's sense of equity, and not its relative competence, that is producing most of the disagreement. Thus, debate over the merits of the jury system is in the end debate over the jury as a means of introducing flexibility and equity into the legal process.

There are, however, some further observations about the issue of jury competence. We have been told often enough that the jury trial is a process whereby twelve inexperienced laymen, who are probably strangers to each other, are invited to apply law which they will not understand to facts which they will not get straight and by secret deliberation arrive at a group decision. We are told also that heroic feats of learning law, remembering facts, and running an orderly discussion as a group are called for in every jury trial. In the forum of armchair speculation, a forum which on this topic has enrolled some of the most able and distinguished names in law, the jury often loses the day.

The two basic tables giving the architectural statistics of the jury's performance vis-à-vis the judge's performance have already indicated that the armchair indictment of the jury must go awry somewhere. We can, however, in a variety of ways document more securely our assertion that intellectual incompetence or sheer misunderstanding of the case is not a problem with the jury.

In the judge-jury survey the trial judge, among other things, classified each case as to whether it was "difficult to understand" or "easy." We can therefore spell out the following hypothesis to test against the judge-jury data. If the jury has a propensity not to understand, that propensity should be more evident in the cases rated by the judges as difficult than in those rated as easy.[22] Further, disagreement should be higher in cases which the jury does not understand than in cases which they do understand since, where the jury misunderstands the case, it must be deciding on a different basis than the judge. We reach, then, the de-

---

22. It might be noted that some 85% of the cases were rated by the judges as falling in the "easy" category.

cisive hypothesis to test, namely, that the jury should disagree more often with the judge in difficult cases than in easy ones. However, when we compare the decision patterns in easy cases with those in difficult cases we find that the level of disagreement remains the same.[23]

This rather intricate proof is corroborated by the fact that although the trial judges polled gave a wide variety of explanations for the cases in which there was disagreement, they virtually never offered the jury's inability to understand the case as a reason.

Different jurors remember, and make available to all, different items of the trial so that the jury as a group remembers far more than most of its members could as individuals. It tends, in this connection, to be as strong as its strongest link. The conclusion, therefore, is that the jury understands well enough for its purposes and that its intellectual incompetence has been vastly exaggerated.

Often in the debate over the jury the capacity of *one* layman is compared to the capacity of one judge, as though this were the issue. The distinctive strength and safeguard of the jury system is that the jury operates as a group. Whether twelve lay heads are better than one judicial head is still open to argument, but it should be recognized that twelve lay heads are very probably better than one.

It has been a major characteristic of debate over the jury that its critics are quick to announce at the outset that they are talking only of civil juries—their argument is not meant to impeach juries in criminal cases. The view I have been developing in this paper sees the jury as an adjudicating institution with certain basic characteristics and qualities which would be relatively constant as its business moves from civil to criminal cases. The question I wish to explore for a moment is the logic by which one would abolish the civil jury and cherish the criminal jury. I recognize, of course, that as a practical matter there are great differences here in terms of both constitutional requirements and popular reaction. I wish, however, to look theoretically at this matter. If the jury operates in a civil case as its critics say, can one justify retaining such an archaic and incompetent institution in criminal cases?

The answer to all this, of course, is likely to be that we favor the jury in criminal cases as a safeguard for the accused, and

23. The data here discussed come from the study of criminal cases; there is no reason to believe the point will not hold for civil trials as well.

that we need no corresponding safeguard in the civil case. There are two things to note about this line of reasoning, however. First, it would seem to be waiving any objections about the jury's incompetence and resting the case on the jury's sense of equity. Second, since it recognizes that introducing equity into the legal scheme is a characteristic of the jury, is there sufficient basis for applauding the jury's brand of equity in criminal cases while being critical of it in civil cases?

.   .   .

It has been a traditional point of argument against the jury that it ameliorated the harsh rules of law just enough to dampen any enthusiasm or momentum toward proper reform. It is easy to say that a rule of law is either sound or unsound. If it is sound it should be enforced as written; if it is unsound it should be changed by proper process. This logical scheme, however, seems to me too rigid. Reform of private law is notoriously hard to effectuate, and in the long interim there is room for the jury's touch. Further, there is not inconsiderable evidence that jury resistance to a rule is often a catalyst of change. Finally, and perhaps most important, we have a sense that many of the jury's most interesting deviations would be exceedingly hard to codify and incorporate by rule.

The content of jury equity in civil cases is obviously a topic of high interest, and we have not yet documented it fully in our studies.

.   .   .

In the end, then, debate about the merits of the jury system should center far more on the value and propriety of the jury's sense of equity, of its modest war with the law, than on its sheer competence. Criticism of the jury raises a deep, durable, and perplexing jurisprudential issue, and not a simple one of the professional engineer versus the amateur.

On most issues of policy one may question the relevance of an opinion poll as an aid to forming his own opinion. In the case of the jury, however, an opinion poll may have extra force. In any event, the final item of data I wish to report is a survey we conducted among a national sample of trial judges as to their opinions of, and attitudes toward, the jury system. The trial judge's views as to the value of the jury are especially entitled to respectful hearing: he is the daily observer of the jury system in action, its daily partner in the administration of justice, and the one who would be most affected if the civil jury were abolished.

The questionnaire was elaborate and reflected a series of specific points about which we had become concerned during the life of the project. When reported in full, it should yield a rounded profile of contemporary judicial attitudes toward the jury and toward specific reforms that might increase its usefulness. At the moment we shall rest with reporting two basic tables. The judges were asked to choose among three positions on the jury for criminal, and then for civil trials:

(1) On balance the jury system is thoroughly satisfactory.

(2) The jury system has serious disadvantages which could be corrected and should be corrected if the system is to remain useful.

(3) The disadvantages of the jury system outweigh its advantages so much that its use should be sharply curtailed.

There were some 1,060 trial judges in the national sample. Table 3 gives the results for criminal cases and Table 4 for civil cases.

Table 3

Trial Judges' Opinions of Jury—Criminal Cases

		Number	Per Cent
(1)	Thoroughly Satisfactory	791	77
(2)	Satisfactory if Certain Changes	210	20
(3)	Unsatisfactory	29	3
		1,030	100

Table 4

Trial Judges' Opinions of Jury—Civil Cases

		Number	Per Cent
(1)	Thoroughly Satisfactory	661	64
(2)	Satisfactory if Certain Changes	280	27
(3)	Unsatisfactory	97	9
		1,038	100

The tables require little comment. It is evident that the trial judges are overwhelmingly against sharp curtailment of the jury; that a substantial majority find the jury thoroughly satisfactory; and that this support for the jury does not decline appreciably as we shift from criminal to civil cases.

. . .

Sometimes I suspect that the jury issue will go to whichever side does not have the burden of proof. And in the forum of policy debate the assignment of the burden of proof tends to be a debater's strategy rather than an accepted convention. Does the argument stand differently if, on the one hand, the issue is put in terms of introducing the civil jury into a system that does not have it or perhaps extending it to areas where we do not have it today, such as the Federal Tort Claims Act, than it does if, on the other hand, the issue is whether we should abolish the jury in areas where we do now have it? I think it does, and I incline toward the view that old institutions should not be changed lightly. . . .

Notes and Questions

1. Some judicial authors also disagree with Judge Frank's views. Judge Bernard Botein, a New York trial judge prior to his promotion to the appellate bench, warmly defended the jury as an institution in his book "Trial Judge" (1952). He noted that although the jury does not always see all the influences and forces that affect their decisions "neither does a judge." Although inexperienced in the courtroom the jury is eager to do its job. Judge Botein found the jury less jaded than the judge who has come to know the lawyers and expert witnesses who appear frequently before him. His negative impressions of these persons may often unfairly prejudice their clients. Also, after several exposures to similar situations a judge's thinking may become routinated and not wholly responsive to the case at hand.

He also asserted that although in cases involving commercial transactions a judge's experience might make him superior to a jury, this was not true in all kinds of cases. In direct credibility conflicts, Judge Botein thought a jury of 12 generally better equipped than he alone to ascertain truth. In mechanical or technical cases, the judge thought it likely that the average jury would include several persons who understood the particular problem better than would the average judge.

Finally, Judge Botein argued that the judge can help restrain any possible prejudice by his control of the flow of information to the jury—and his subsequent power to upset jury verdicts that seem palpably mistaken. The most troublesome problem he saw was that of a broadly based community prejudice that would not cancel out in the jury room.

Perhaps his position is best summarized by the following statement: "Juries are excellent, good, bad, and indifferent—much like judges."

In recent years, Judge Botein has cooperated in the preparation of motion pictures and handbooks for the orientation of jurors. He initiated procedures that boost the morale of jurors by using their time more efficiently, a particularly acute problem in urban jurisdictions.

2. Are Kalven's figures persuasive in establishing that when judge and jury disagree, the explanation is not incompetence but rather the jury's "sense of equity" or its different views of credibility?

3. Do you view jury "legislation" as an asset or a liability of the jury system? Is your answer the same for both civil and criminal cases?

4. Does the jury's character as a cross-section of the community help avoid the social biases of the judge and possible judicial arbitrariness? Is this equally important in both civil and criminal cases?

5. Do juries further the goal of "equal justice under law?" If not, should they be abolished in all cases? Only in civil cases?

6. There is a split in our courts about whether during his charge, the judge may tell the jury his impressions of witnesses and which ones he believed. The advice is not binding on the jury but is only one man's opinion of credibility. Should this practice be encouraged? Should it be prohibited?

That the Towle jury paid substantial attention to the judge's instructions and that they were talking about important evidence is suggested by the following episode that took place 30 minutes after the jury had retired.

(Jury returns. 11:40 a.m.)

The Clerk: Mr. Johnson, as foreman of the Jury, do you have a verdict to report at this time?

Mr. Johnson: No, we have not. We have a question. We would like to hear some of the evidence pertaining to the sheriff's letter, in which he said, "To Whom it May Concern."

The Court: Mrs. Alexander, could you read that portion of the testimony? I believe it occurred in the cross-examination of Sheriff Finn by Mr. Lisman.

(The following questions and answers from the cross-examination of Sheriff Finn by Mr. Lisman were read by the reporter.)

"Q. This has been identified as being under your own signature and under your own handwriting?

A. Has it? I believe so. It is my letter.

Q. Does it start off, 'December 3, 1957. To Whom it May Concern: Ronald Towle was never suspended from the Franklin County Sheriff's Patrol for violation of organizational rules'?

A. That is what it says.

Q. It is in your handwriting?

A. That is correct.

Q. And it is signed by you?

A. That is correct."

The Court: Now, Mr. Johnson, is there any more of the testimony that you wish read concerning . . .

Mr. Johnson: Is that part of the evidence?

The Court: The letter itself was not offered as an exhibit and, therefore, the letter itself is not available to the jury. However, the verbal testimony concerning the contents of the letter which Mrs. Alexander just read to you is available to you.

Mr. Deming: Should I speak to him or speak directly to you? (Juror) I mean, I want to ask another question.

The Court: I think it would be best, why doesn't the jury retire and—

Mr. Deming: It is regarding something in this testimony.

The Court: Why don't you take it up in the jury room and then Mr. Johnson can make another request of the Court. We will see then if we can't straighten it out in a more orderly fashion.

(Jury retires to the Jury Room)

————

The jury thereupon returned to its deliberations. How long will it deliberate before reaching a verdict? There is no minimum or maximum time limit; juries have returned with verdicts barely minutes after having retired. There are also cases in which the jury may deliberate at great length but be unable to reach agreement. These cases result in a so-called "hung jury," and must be tried again before different jurors. Unfortunately, but understandably, juries tend to disagree in the more lengthy and complex law suits, making a re-trial costly in terms of time and money. Typically, the judge will ask a jury that reports disagreement to try again in the hope of avoiding a retrial, but eventually if the jury cannot reach a verdict it will be discharged.

What does it mean to say "reach a verdict?" Is a vote of 7 to 5 sufficient? Until recently, Anglo-American law generally required that jury verdicts be unanimous, either to convict or acquit, in most criminal trials. The United Kingdom made a major change in 1967 to permit a majority verdict of at least 10 to 2 in all criminal cases provided that

> A court shall not accept a majority verdict unless it appears to the court that the jury have had not less than two hours for deliberation or such longer period as the court thinks reasonable having regard to the nature and complexity of the case.

What are the arguments for and against this change in the law? Is a defendant in a criminal case more protected by the requirement that his guilt be proven beyond a reasonable doubt, or that the jury be unanimous?

In civil cases some states adhere to the unanimity requirement while others require a majority of only three-fourths or five-sixths. The latter believe that to require unanimity would unduly impede the resolution of cases in which the consequences to the loser are generally less serious than in criminal cases and in which *some* resolution in one attempt may be preferable to a series of trials to gain a unanimous verdict.

That Vermont followed the unanimity rule was no problem in the Towle case. At 2:43 P.M. that afternoon, presumably with time out for lunch, the jury returned to the courtroom and the following exchange took place.

The Clerk: Mr. Johnson, as foreman of this jury do you have a verdict to report at this time?

Mr. Johnson: We do.

(Plaintiff's Verdict, $3500.)

The Clerk: Is this your verdict, Mr. Foreman?

Mr. Johnson: It is.

The Clerk: So say you all, Ladies and Gentlemen of the Jury?

(Jury answer in affirmative)

The Court: The verdict may be noted.

(Jury dismissed)

Mr. Lisman: At this time the plaintiff moves for judgment on the verdict.

The Court:	Your request is noted, Mr. Lisman.
Mr. Mulvey:	I would like leave to file written motions in connection with setting the verdict aside.
The Court:	We will allow you until Friday, October 2, 1959 to file any motions that you might have.
Mr. Lisman:	And action on our motion for judgment will of course be delayed until that time?
The Court:	Delayed until that time.

The ambiguity of a general verdict is now clear. We do not know whether the jury found the second story to be true or false because the $3,500 might have been the jury's assessment of damages incurred from the first story or it might have been the combined damages from both stories. Similarly, we do not know whether this amount included specific items such as the loss on the house sale or is only a general award for reputational harm. Nor do we know whether the jury did disregard loss of promotion damages, for the admonition to do so might only have drawn it to their attention. Such ambiguity may be surprising, but the overwhelming percentage of jury verdicts are in this general form.

The jury is now dismissed and, since the court will act only if a litigant takes the initiative, Mr. Lisman makes a motion asking the judge to implement the verdict by awarding the plaintiff $3,500. Mr. Mulvey, however, unhappy with the verdict, needs time to file written motions.

It is rare that both sides are satisfied with the verdict, and occasionally, both are dissatisfied. If Mr. Lisman, for example, had thought the case was worth $10,000, he might be even less happy with the jury verdict than is Mr. Mulvey. The problem to which we soon turn is how attorneys indicate their displeasure with various aspects of the trial and the verdict.

R. TRIAL WITHOUT JURY

As we have seen, Vermont granted the right to trial by jury in this case. England, which abolished the right to a jury in almost all civil cases in 1933, preserved that right in defamation cases. Is there greater reason to preserve the right to a jury in defamation cases than, for example, automobile accident cases?

In fact the right of jury trial is exercised in the overwhelming majority of defamation cases.

It will be instructive, however, to consider how the Towle trial would have developed had the parties waived a jury trial. One careful study estimates that the average non-jury trial would be 40% briefer than a jury trial of the same case. This time is saved by not having to pick or charge a jury and eliminating post-trial motions and, in many cases, opening and closing statements. The entire spirit is much more informal with fewer objections to evidence and no histrionics. Although the defenses of the jury system quoted earlier were not addressed to the delay point, Professor Kalven asserts that the problems of congestion and delay can be handled by other techniques without altering the basic "quality of our justice."

Perhaps the most important difference between the two types of trial occurs when, at the end, the judge takes the case under advisement. He does not retire to his chambers as does a jury. He forms impressions at the trial, takes notes, (a practice sometimes forbidden to jurors) and then within a few weeks will issue his decision. This decision will contain "findings of fact" that will approximate a jury's special verdict on every important fact. We will learn which witnesses he believed on which points. He will then present his "conclusions of law," a statement of the relevant rules and their application to the facts. Thus, if an appeal is taken, the reviewing court will know precisely what happened at the trial and why.

––––––––––

S. THE JUDGE AGREES WITH THE JURY

You will recall that Mr. Mulvey asked for time in which to file motions attacking the verdict. These motions are of two kinds. The first is a motion in which the party who lost before the jury makes a "motion for judgment notwithstanding the verdict" (usually abbreviated "judgment n. o. v." for judgment *non obstante veredicto*). This motion is essentially a delayed motion for a directed verdict. Where the motion for a directed verdict asked the judge to keep the case from the jury because only one result could reasonably be reached, the judgment n. o. v. motion contends that the jury has indeed reached an "impossible" result and asks the judge to rule that the moving party is entitled to win the case now just as he would have had a directed verdict been rendered.

The utility of this motion is explicable in terms of the trial judge's predicament. Suppose he thinks that the case is so heavily weighted on the defendant's side that the jury couldn't reasonably find for the plaintiff. Technically this would justify his granting a directed verdict, but if he does so and an appellate court decides he was wrong then the whole case will have to be retried. This induces many judges to deny a motion for a directed verdict even when they think the defendant may be legally entitled to it. The case then goes to the jury, and all is well if their verdict accords with his views. If, however, the judge still believes that the jury's verdict is clearly unsound he now grants judgment n. o. v. Even if he is wrong no retrial will be necessary because a jury has already been heard from and the appellate court can simply order that verdict reinstated. Since it is difficult to be certain whether the evidence warrants a directed verdict, judges often prefer to hear the jury's view before acting.

The second type of post-trial motion is less sweeping: the losing party asks only for a "new trial" (rather than an absolute victory). This motion asks the trial judge to take a second look at what happened during the trial and to rectify any serious mistakes he might now think he made. If the judge, for example, should later think that he erred in permitting introduction of a piece of evidence that probably accounted for either the plaintiff's victory or the size of the verdict, he will grant a new trial. If he has just learned that the jury reached its verdict by flipping a coin, or other improper procedure, he may call for a new trial. If the losing party has just discovered some important new evidence that it could not reasonably have found before the trial, the judge may order a new trial. Finally, the trial judge might set aside the verdict and order a new trial where, although he recognizes that the jury could "reasonably" have decided the case either way, he has an abiding sense that the jury reached the "wrong" result. To take an extreme example, if the plaintiff presents only one witness, a convicted murderer or the town drunk, to testify that the defendant in an automobile accident had the red light, that is enough to permit the jury to find that fact if they believe the witness. But suppose the defendant in that case presents ten clergymen who also claim to be eye-witnesses and who testify that the defendant had a green light. Assume there is no other evidence. This is a classic credibility dispute to be resolved by the jury; either outcome would be within reason. In such a case if the jury decided for the plaintiff the judge could not enter a judgment n. o. v. for the defendant because there is competent evidence to support the plaintiff's contentions. The trial judge might decide, however, based on his perceptions of the witnesses, that the verdict is so heavily "against the weight of the evidence" that he will grant a new trial to hear what a second jury has to say. If the second jury comes to the same conclusions as the first, the trial judge will almost certainly allow that verdict to stand and conclude that the jurors' assessment of who was telling the truth was sounder than his. In this type of situation the judge is often said to function as a "thirteenth juror."

Within the time limit given him by Judge Hill, Mr. Mulvey filed the following motion:

MOTION TO SET ASIDE THE VERDICT AND FOR JUDGMENT NOTWITHSTANDING THE VERDICT

Now comes the Defendant, by its Attorney, and moves that the verdict in the above case be set aside and that judgment be entered for the Defendant notwithstanding the verdict. The grounds of said Motion are:

1. The verdict as rendered is against the weight of the evidence.

2. There is no competent evidence in the case upon which the jury could have based its verdict.

3. The verdict in the amount of Thirty-Five Hundred Dollars ($3500.00) is excessive as there is no competent evidence that the Plaintiff suffered damages in such an amount.

WHEREFORE, the Defendant moves that the verdict be set aside and judgment be entered for it.

Dated at St. Albans City, this 1st day of October, 1959.

ST. ALBANS PUBLISHING CO., INC.

BY /s/ John Mulvey

Its Attorney

———

Mr. Mulvey's motion is apparently a combination of the two types we have discussed. The first point would seem to suggest that defendant is asking for a new trial, but the second point, emphasizing as it does "no competent evidence", asks that the plaintiff's case be thrown out once and for all—a motion for judgment n. o. v. The third point, about damages, seems to ask only for a new trial.

If Judge Hill had concluded that the jury was correct in finding the defendant liable, but that they awarded the plaintiff an
unreasonably large sum, the judge could have handled this by
giving the plaintiff a choice of either facing a new trial or of
remitting the portion of the award that the judge thinks is in
excess of what a reasonable jury might have awarded. In fact,
however, Mr. Mulvey's motion was denied without opinion by
the court which then, again without opinion, granted Mr. Lisman's motion made at the end of the trial that judgment be entered "on the verdict." The court apparently concluded that the
verdict was sound and issued the following document:

JUDGMENT ORDER

Judgment is hereby entered that the plaintiff recover of the
defendant the sum of Three Thousand Five Hundred Dollars
($3,500.00) together with costs, which costs are taxed and al-
lowed at Twenty-nine Dollars ($29.00).

Dated this 20th day of October, 1959.

/s/ William C. Hill
_____

_____
/s/ Louis G. LaValley

———

Who is Louis G. LaValley? Mr. LaValley was one of two
assistant judges who sat with Judge Hill throughout the trial.
In colonial times laymen were elected to these posts to help control the distrusted judiciary. Only in Vermont is this usage
retained today. Theoretically, all decisions are by majority
vote, so that Judge Hill might have been outvoted on any issue.
In practice, however, the assistant judges defer to the trained
jurist on questions of law and their primary role is to help the
judge decide fact questions in cases tried without a jury. Here
they often outvote the judge on such issues as credibility. Only
two votes are needed for action so the other assistant judge's
signature was not required on the judgment order. This unique
practice also explains the use of "we" by Judge Hill at several
places in the transcript.

This "judgment" is the culmination of the trial court procedure. The "verdict" is only the action of a jury while the
"judgment" is what really matters—the decision of the court.
There is now on record a judicial declaration that the plaintiff
is entitled to recover $3,500 from the defendant.

Notice, however, that the judgment does not literally order the defendant personally to do anything. It says only that the plaintiff shall recover this money. It is now up to the defendant to take the next step. After consideration of the possible grounds for reversal and the costs of appealing, defendant decided to appeal.

T. THE APPELLATE STRUCTURE

In this country we so often hear the phrase, "I'll appeal this to the highest court," that we tend to take for granted the presence of an appellate system, but it would not be irrational for a legal system to declare that the Towle case was now finished. Indeed, in some specific kinds of cases both the English and American legal systems do precisely that: entitle the parties to one hearing, or trial, with no possibility of an appeal. At this stage in our legal development, however, we recognize the desirability if not the need for appellate review in ordinary cases. Our sense of justice is not satisfied by relying upon the unreviewable rulings of a single judge. This is especially true as legal problems become more complex. Though it is possible for the losing party, by a motion for new trial, to ask the trial judge to reconsider alleged errors he has made, the judge may lack the objectivity to review his own decisions.

Smaller states generally have only one appellate court, usually with five or seven justices and almost always called the Supreme Court. (Members of the highest court in a system are often called "justices" while all others are "judges.") Vermont, for example, has only one appellate court, a five-member "Supreme Court."

The more populous states may have two appellate levels. Litigants may generally appeal cases from the trial court to a three-or-five judge intermediate appellate court whose decisions may then be appealed to the state's highest court, usually a Supreme Court, with seven or nine justices. In such a three-level system the Supreme Court usually has great discretion in deciding which cases to accept from the intermediate court. They are required to grant review in certain kinds of cases, such as those involving constitutional problems, and may pick from among the rest according to the importance of the issues presented.

Some states faced with a growing number of appeals have attempted to handle them without creating an intermediate appellate court system. In these states the Supreme Court is authorized to divide itself into two panels with the decisions of one such panel tantamount to that of the full court. A state with a seven-member Supreme Court might divide itself into two four-man panels, with the Chief Justice being the fourth member of each panel. Very difficult or important cases will be heard by the entire court.

The federal system at first provided essentially for only one appeal—to the Supreme Court of the United States. In 1891, however, Congress created several multi-state units, or "circuits," to provide an intermediate appellate system. Thus, for example, cases decided in the federal district courts of New York, Connecticut and Vermont may all be appealed to the United States Court of Appeals for the Second Circuit, which includes nine judges from those three states. The nine, however, sit in panels of three except in the most important cases, when all sit "en banc". There are now eleven such circuits throughout the country.

In 1925 the Supreme Court sought, and received, from Congress vast discretion over which court of appeals cases should get another review. The Court had to go to Congress because Article III of the Constitution, after defining the Supreme Court's "original jurisdiction" (those cases in which the Supreme Court functions as a trial court, such as in disputes between two states), provides in Section 2 that "in all other Cases, . . . the Supreme Court shall have appellate Jurisdiction . . . with such Exceptions, and under such Regulations as the Congress shall make."

The net result of the 1925 statute is that cases being brought to the Supreme Court from the lower federal courts fall into two categories. A very few are "appeals" that the Court *must* hear and decide; the overwhelming majority of cases are reviewed only if the Court grants the litigant's petition for a "writ of certiorari." Supreme Court Rule 19, written by the Court, provides the following guidance for litigants who have lost in the court of appeals and do not have the type of case the Supreme Court is obligated to hear by "appeal":

> A review on writ of certiorari is not a matter of right, but of sound judicial discretion, and will be granted only where there are special and important reasons therefor. The following, while neither controlling nor fully measuring the court's discretion, indicate the character of reasons which will be considered:
>
> . . .
>
> (b) Where a court of appeals has rendered a decision in conflict with the decision of another court of

appeals on the same matter; or has decided an important state or territorial question in a way in conflict with applicable state or territorial law; or has decided an important question of federal law which has not been, but should be, settled by this court; or has decided a federal question in a way in conflict with applicable decisions of this court; or has so far departed from the accepted and usual course of judicial proceedings, or so far sanctioned such a departure by a lower court, as to call for an exercise of this court's power of supervision.

The party seeking the writ of certiorari files a petition setting forth his reasons why the Court should hear the case. The other party then may counter that the case does not come within the guidelines of Rule 19 and does not merit discretionary acceptance. After considering the papers the Court will simply announce without explanation or opinion whether or not it has decided to hear the case.

The late Fred Vinson, Chief Justice of the United States (1946–53)—this is his correct title; he is *not* Chief Justice of the Supreme Court—once said that far too many petitions for certiorari "reveal a serious misconception on the part of counsel concerning the role of the Supreme Court. . . . Lawyers might be well advised, in preparing petitions for certiorari, to spend a little less time discussing the merits and a little more time demonstrating why it is important the Court should hear them." The import of Chief Justice Vinson's remarks and those of other justices is that the denial of a petition for certiorari does not imply any view on the merits of the case; it can properly be understood only as an indication that fewer than four members of the Supreme Court thought the case worth hearing. It is interesting to note that the discretionary jurisdiction of the United States Supreme Court may be invoked by fewer than a majority of its nine members. If four of the nine think that the case should be heard, it will be heard. Are you concerned about the likelihood that the Supreme Court leaves standing some lower court decisions that may be "wrong"? How can this action be justified?

U. THE APPELLATE PROCESS

We turn now from the structure of the appellate system to its operation. The general principle is that no party may appeal unless a "final judgment" has been entered with which he is dissatisfied.   Each party during a lawsuit must accumulate all claimed errors until the case is concluded in favor of one party or the other.   Until that stage we cannot tell whether the party who wants to appeal will really have a grievance.   If, for example, Sgt. Towle's attorney had been barred from introducing certain evidence, he could not stop the trial and take an appeal; if Sgt. Towle were to win the trial even without that evidence, he would have nothing to complain about.   On the other hand, if Sgt. Towle's case had been dismissed because the judge thought that the statute of limitations had run, that would be a final judgment adverse to Sgt. Towle and he could appeal immediately. The general principle of delaying appeals until we see who won may, however, become wasteful.   If Mr. Mulvey had moved to dismiss Sgt. Towle's complaint as barred by the statute of limitations, but the trial judge disagreed, is it desirable to require a complete trial before appealing that ruling?   If Mr. Mulvey is right, the case should be ended right now, rather than after a full trial.   All court systems provide for "interlocutory" appeals when it is thought that the benefits of quick appeal outweigh the disadvantages.

In the actual Towle case, when Judge Hill ruled that Sgt. Towle was entitled to recover $3,500, that was a final judgment in the Chittenden County Court and an appeal became permissible. Sgt. Towle was satisfied and planned no appeal.

How soon must the defendant appeal?   This matter is regulated by statute in all appellate systems.   In Vermont, within 30 days the appealing party (the appellant) must file a document called a "Notice of Appeal" which must "specify the parties taking the appeal, designate the judgment. . . and be signed by the party appealing or his attorney."   Within the 30 days, on November 14, 1959, Mr. Mulvey filed the following notice of appeal.

November 14, 1959

Re: Ronald Towle vs. St. Albans
       Publishing Company, Inc.
       Chittenden County

Dear Mr. Rousseau:

Notice is hereby given that the Defendant hereby appeals from the judgment order in the above captioned case (Ronald Towle vs. St. Albans Publishing Company, Inc). This judgment order is dated October 20, 1959 and is in words and figures as follows:

> "Judgment is hereby entered that the plaintiff receives of the defendant the sum of Three Thousand Five Hundred Dollars ($3,500) together with costs which costs are taxed and allowed at twenty-nine dollars ($29)"—

This appeal is taken to the Supreme Court of the State of Vermont and is from the Chittenden County Court.

I have previously paid you the entry fee of $5 which you have acknowledged. Copies of this letter are enclosed for Norman Peduzzi, Clerk of the General Term of the Supreme Court and Lisman & Lisman, attorneys for the plaintiff.

Very truly yours,

/s/ John Mulvey

Now that Mr. Mulvey has met the formal requirements he must get down to the hard work of preparing his appeal. His approach is determined by what he knows about the Vermont Supreme Court's function. First, it is solely an appellate court; it does not see witnesses or hear new evidence, nor hold anything resembling a trial. It is interested only in reviewing the actions of the trial judge. There is much truth in the common observation that "the trial judge tries the case, and the appellate court tries the trial judge." The appealing party, the appellant, must file a "brief," a document in which the attorney cites the allegedly erroneous rulings of the trial judge and supports his claims by legal arguments. The opposing party (the "appellee" or the "respondent") files a "brief" arguing that the trial judge was correct in these rulings.

In order to make his points the appellant must make clear to the Supreme Court what happened in the trial court. If Mr. Mulvey wants to argue that the plaintiff's complaint was barred by the statute of limitations he must at least give the court a copy of the complaint. Similarly, if Mr. Mulvey wishes to complain about certain evidence allowed at the trial he must provide a transcript, or at least those passages from the transcript that are relevant. All material collected from the lower court proceedings that is submitted to the appellate court is called the "record" or "record on appeal." Since the Towle trial was short, this record included the entire trial transcript. In a long and complicated case the parties may agree that only limited parts of the proceedings need be submitted.

Appellate courts primarily review *legal* rulings by the lower court judges. They are concerned with whether the judge properly stated and applied the law in his several rulings—whether on adequacy of the complaint, or admission of evidence—and in his charge to the jury. The appellate judges will "reverse" the case and send it back to the lower court for further action if they decide that the trial judge has committed "prejudicial error". If an appellate court reversed every time the trial judge made a mistake, very few cases would ever be "affirmed." Therefore, they look only for error that is likely to have prejudiced a party and contributed to the contested result. This type of error is referred to as "prejudicial" or "reversible" error.

In addition to reviewing legal questions, however, the appellate court may review fact determinations made by the jury. If Mr. Mulvey thinks that the jury's findings were unsupported on a particular ground, he may raise this on appeal. Note, however, that generally he will raise it by a claim that the judge had erred in not setting the jury's verdict aside. (In criminal cases there is no appeal from a jury verdict of acquittal.)

Although an appellate court reviewing the trial judge's legal rulings will reverse if it finds prejudicial error, its review of the trial judge's rulings on *facts* is much more restricted; it will ask only whether the jury could reasonably have decided the way it did. Our reliance on juries indicates that we think they are better judges of credibility than the trial judge. If true at the trial, this is more valid on appeal where the judges have not even seen the witnesses.

Finally, Mr. Mulvey may argue that the trial judge should have given him a new trial because, although sufficient, the plaintiff's evidence was heavily outweighed by the defendant's evidence—as in the example of the convicted murderer's testimony against that of ten clergymen. You will recall that Judge Hill, in his role of "thirteenth juror," disagreed with Mr. Mulvey's assessment of the evidence and therefore denied Mr. Mulvey's post-trial motion for a new trial. If Mr. Mulvey wishes to raise this argument again he must show not merely that the trial judge was "wrong" but that he "abused his discretion" in failing to give the defendant a new trial. In other words Mr. Mulvey must show that the trial judge was not merely wrong but very, very wrong.

To sum up, appellate courts use three distinct standards in deciding appeals. First, on all legal rulings the issue will be whether the trial judge committed prejudicial error. On the question of whether the trial judge correctly decided the defendant's motion for judgment n. o. v., the issue will be whether a jury could reasonably have found for the plaintiff. On the third matter, whether the trial judge correctly denied the defendant's motion for a new trial because the verdict was against the weight of the evidence, the issue will be whether the trial judge abused his discretion in deciding the motion. (If the trial judge sat without a jury his findings of fact will be upset on appeal only if the appellate court thinks them "clearly erroneous.")

This will become clearer as we read the Towle opinion. The important point to recognize now is that this imposes a heavy burden on the lawyer who is handling the appeal. Mr. Mulvey recognized this and knew that it would be costly for his client to take an appeal. Therefore, before he started work on the appeal the following exchange of letters took place.

December 8, 1959

Re: Towle vs. St. Albans Publishing Co., Inc.

Dear Louie:

As you know, I have ordered a transcript in the above case and all steps preliminary to the appeal are now completed. However, the hard work is yet to come, so if there is any possibility of settling this case for say $2000, would you let me know before I make my briefs. I am not saying that my client would have $2000 if you were to agree, but I will say that I would recommend that they try to raise this amount immediately. Let me hear from you.

Yours truly,

/s/ John Mulvey

December 10, 1959

Re: Ronald Towle vs. St. Albans Publishing Co.

Dear John:

I doubt very much that my client would be interested in a settlement of $2,000. However, I have written him and put it entirely up to his judgment.

I shall be in touch with you again as soon as I hear from him.

Sincerely yours,

/s/ Louis Lisman

By telephone, Mr. Lisman subsequently told Mr. Mulvey that though Sgt. Towle had earlier been willing to accept $2,000 he no longer was. Under what circumstances might Towle have accepted the $2,000 offer at this stage? Mr. Mulvey then began work on the appeal. In reading Mr. Mulvey's brief that follows, focus primarily on the form of presentation and the techniques used rather than on the merits of the various arguments.

STATE OF VERMONT

RONALD W. TOWLE VS. ST. ALBANS PUBLISHING CO., INC.	SUPREME COURT CHITTENDEN COUNTY

DEFENDANT'S BRIEF

This is an action claiming damage for alleged libelous publication. The defendant is the owner of the *St. Albans Messenger,* a daily newspaper published in St. Albans. At the times material, the plaintiff was a sergeant in the Air Force and was a resident of Fairfax, Vermont. At the time suit was brought, he was a resident of Milton, Vermont. In connection with his Air Force duties he was assigned to the Air Police. Previous to the publication of the alleged libels, he was a member of the Franklin County Sheriff's Patrol and acted as a law enforcement officer.

Prior to his enlistment in the Air Force, the plaintiff had been before a resident of the County. On May 28, 1941 he was charged with Careless and Negligent Operation of a Motor Vehicle resulting in the death of one Elwood. On June 16, 1941 he pleaded "Nolo" to the charge and was adjudged guilty, to serve eight to twelve months in the House of Correction and to pay a fine of $100 and costs. The prison sentence was suspended. All facts regarding the sentence were excluded from evidence.

In connection with this offense, the plaintiff's right to operate a motor vehicle was suspended, and, before it was reinstated, he was required to file personal responsibility insurance. He subsequently left the State and acquired a Virginia license. When he returned to Vermont he did not file the required insurance with the Commissioner and consequently did not have a right to drive in Vermont. During part of this time he was a member of the Sheriff's Patrol and did operate his motor vehicle.

During the plaintiff's tenure as a member of the Sheriff's Patrol, complaints regarding his conduct were received by the Sheriff, and the Sheriff discontinued making use of him. (Tr. 55) About this time, or shortly thereafter, the Air Force issued an order directing its personnel to discontinue certain law enforcement activities. (Tr. 16) ["Tr." refers to original transcript pagination.]

On November 25, 1957 the plaintiff was arrested for operating a motor vehicle while his right to do so was suspended. To this charge in Franklin Municipal Court, the plaintiff pleaded guilty and was sentenced to pay a fine and costs. On that day the following appeared in the *St. Albans Messenger*:

> "Ronald Towle of Fairfax, an air policeman, formerly of Enosburg, pleaded guilty to driving while intoxicated. He paid a fine of $50 and costs of $12.30."

Part of the news item was the result of an error as it stated that the charge was "driving while intoxicated" when it should have stated "driving while his license was suspended." (Tr. 46)

The following day the newspaper published the following:

[The brief quotes the second article in full.]

Thereupon, the plaintiff brought suit. The defendant, in its answer, admitted the error in its publication of November 25, 1957 but stated in explanation thereof that it was an inadvertent mistake. It further pleaded that the publication of November 26, 1957 was true.

During the trial certain evidence offered by the defendant was excluded over the objection of the defendant. Certain evidence was admitted by the Court over the objection and exception of the defendant. The defendant also objected to the Court's failure to strike certain evidence and objected and took exception to parts of the charge and to the Court's failure to charge. The jury returned a verdict for $3500. Before judgment, the defendant moved to set aside the judgment on the grounds, among others, that the verdict was excessive. The motion was denied and exceptions allowed. This appeal was then taken.

ARGUMENT

For the sake of simplicity, the argument is divided among the following topics:

I EVIDENCE EXCLUDED IN ERROR
    A. Right to cross-examine party.
    B. Right to have certified copy of Court record admitted in evidence.

II EVIDENCE ADMITTED IN ERROR
    A. Plaintiff's Exhibit 1—Letter from Commissioner to plaintiff.
    B. Plaintiff's Exhibit 4—Letter from Douglas C. Decker to plaintiff.
    C. Evidence as to claimed damage as a result of sale of house. (Tr. 25–61)

III FAILURE OF COURT TO CHARGE THE JURY AS REQUESTED
    A. Consideration as to whether the crime committed and the crime published had the same gravity or criminality.
    B. Jury should have been instructed to consider in mitigation of damage and to rebut malice, that the publication of November 25 charging driving while intoxicated was the result of an inadvertent mistake.

IV IT WAS ERROR FOR THE COURT NOT TO SET ASIDE THE VERDICT ON THE GROUND THAT THE DAMAGES WERE EXCESSIVE.

I EVIDENCE EXCLUDED IN ERROR
A. Right to cross-examine plaintiff re previous sentence.

It is a generally recognized rule of law that under our practice a party may be broadly cross-examined in regard to the issues in the case, in regard to credibility, and in regard to matters which might mitigate damages. Knight v. Willey, 120 Vt. 256 at 261.

It has also been held by the Vermont Supreme Court that a party might be compelled to testify to facts which show him guilty of a crime provided that at the time the evidence is given he cannot be prosecuted for the crime. Childs v. Merrill, 66 Vt. 302 Headnote 2.

Furthermore, this action was for a claimed libel wherein the plaintiff claims his character, reputation and credit were injured. The right to damages for an alleged defamatory publication is grounded in injury to reputation. 33 Am.Jur. Libel & Slander 204.

The defendant, by its publication of November 26, reported, among other things, that the plaintiff had been convicted of careless and negligent driving, death resulting. In an action for defamation, the reputation and character of the plaintiff are put in issue by him as he claims injury in that regard. In mitigation of damages, the publication regarding this crime was, of course, put into evidence by the plaintiff (Plaintiff's Exhibit 3). The defendant began cross-examining the plaintiff in regard to the sentence imposed. On Page 29 of the transcript Mr. Lisman for the plaintiff states:

"I object to any evidence of a sentence."

The Court excluded the question. The defendant began again to question the plaintiff:

"If the record were to show you were in . . ."

The Court, on objection, excluded all questions relative to sentence. The defendant made his offer of proof on Page 30 of the transcript, but all questions in this regard were foreclosed. We contend it is reversible error for the Court to exclude these questions.

In cases of defamation it would seem that evidence of good or bad character and standing in the community is generally admissible. Kidder v. Bacon, 74 Vt. 262, Para. 4 at 273; Bowen v. Hall, 20 Vt. 232 at 242–243.

It is respectfully submitted that the plaintiff was more than a witness but was a party and evidence of a prior prison sentence would have been of some weight in mitigating and assessing damages.

B. It was error to exclude the certified copy of the plaintiff's criminal court record.

Attention is called to Page 44 of the transcript. The plaintiff identified a certified copy of the plaintiff's court record. This was offered in connection with the defendant's answer and with the testimony of the plaintiff and in mitigation of damages, having in mind the plaintiff's claimed injury to his reputation and character. The record was excluded and exception allowed. It is respectfully suggested that to exclude the record was prejudicial error. This certified copy was from a court of record, the court being required to keep such records. V. S. A. T 4—Sec. 643 [4 Vt. Statutes Annotated § 643].

The following statute would make this type of evidence admissible if it were otherwise pertinent. This statute provides that certified copies of documents which are required to be kept *shall* be competent evidence. V.S.A. T 12—Sec. 1692.

This Court has allowed cross-examination in regard to crimes committed by a witness even though the record was not in fact produced and in cases not directly involving claimed injury to reputation, such as a libel case. McGovern v. Hays, 75 Vt. 104 at 108.

Allowing admission of such evidence in defamation cases is based on the theory that less damages are in fact suffered if at the time of the claimed injury the plaintiff's reputation has already been impaired. The scope of cross-examination in collateral matters is in the discretion of the Court, but the reputation, character and conduct of the plaintiff prior to the alleged defamation are directly in issue and denying cross-examination in this regard is the denial of a fundamental right. 43 A.L.R. 890; Wigmore Evidence, 2nd Ed. Volume 2 Sec. 1270; 33 Am. Jur., Libel & Slander Sec. 285.

II EVIDENCE ADMITTED IN ERROR

A. Plaintiff's Exhibit 1

This was a letter purporting to be from the Commissioner of Motor Vehicles to the plaintiff referring to a conversation between the Commissioner and the plaintiff and expressing the opinion that the charge of driving while under suspension was a technical charge in this instance. The letter appears in full on Page 45 of the transcript. The objection made by the defendant to the admissibility of this letter appears in the transcript on Page 38 and the exception taken is as follows:

> "May we have an exception on the ground that this is strictly hearsay. I don't have the right to examine the sender of it. Secondly, it is self serving. Number three (it) itself contains hearsay."

B. Plaintiff's Exhibit 4

It is submitted that the admission of this piece of documentary evidence over the defendant's objections was reversible error. This purported to be a letter from one Decker to the plaintiff. Decker did not appear in Court, and the contents of the letter were made available to the jury.

A portion of the letter appears on Page 41 of the transcript:

> "You know, I would sure hate to have a beer bottle for a tube in my radio."

The admission of this letter was objected to on the ground that it was hearsay, the alleged sender was not available for cross-examination, and its admission would be prejudicial. These objections were overruled. (Tr. 40 and 41)

It is respectfully submitted that it was prejudicial error to admit these letters. Both were in effect written statements of Mr. Decker and the Commissioner, if they did send the letters, which had the effect of making them witnesses although they were not present and the contents could not be attacked through either of them.

The following statute was in effect at the time of the trial and was not complied with in any respect.

T 12 § 1609 ADMISSIBILITY OF WRITTEN STATEMENTS

In civil cases, a written statement of a witness, other than when required by law, shall not be admissible in any court proceeding, either as an admission or as impeaching evidence, unless such written statement is taken pursuant to the requirements for depositions provided in chapter 29 of this title, or unless, before offering such statement in evidence, the party offering the same identifies the person and capacity of the person taking the same and the circumstances under which the same was taken.

However, should the statute not apply, the common law rules regarding the admission of hearsay evidence were clearly violated. The purported letter from the Commissioner stated in substance that in his opinion the violation of law in regard to operating a motor vehicle while under suspension was not a serious one and thus had the effect of enhancing the plaintiff's character and making his guilt not serious. Cross-examination of the Commissioner might have been effective to change this, but the defendant was denied the chance.

A case which lays down the rule of law in this regard was decided in Vermont in 1879. It too was a libel action and, over objection, a paper attesting the good character of the plaintiff was received.

The Court stated on Page 520 of Volume 51:

"We think the evidence was inadmissible. Witnesses who are to testify to facts material to the inquiry of the Court must appear in Court where they can be seen and cross-examined.

Shurtleff v. Stevens, 51 Vt. 501 at 520.

Also see Wilkin v. Metcalf, 71 Vt. 103 at 108 where a letter from a third person containing statements made by the plaintiff was held to have been properly excluded.

These letters were not in any way authenticated so there is no proof that they were in fact sent by those who purportedly signed them. See Authentication of Private Writings, 20 Am. Jur. Evidence Sec. 955.

C. Evidence regarding damages in sale of plaintiff's Fairfax House (Tr. 25–36–61)

In substance, the testimony was that the plaintiff bought the house in 1954 for $4000. He and his family lived in it until 1958 when he sold it for $4500. He stated that after he had bought it he had improved it to the value of $1500 thus making an investment in the house of $5500.

The defendant moved to strike the evidence regarding this matter as there was no connecting proof that the plaintiff had to sell the house as a result of the libel and that the damages were speculative. (Tr. 62)

It should be noted that this item of damage was not pleaded in the declaration. The fact that a man would sell his house because of a publication which charges that he committed one crime when in fact he had committed another and that he was dropped from the Sheriff's Patrol for misuse of authority (which the Sheriff stated was true. Tr. 54) is not a natural consequence and unforeseeable. The principle involved is stated in the texts in the following manners:

> "The principle that damages may be recovered only for such injuries as flow directly from and are the probable and natural result of the wrong complained of necessarily excludes all those consequences of the act which are remote and indirect and all investigation of losses which are purely speculative."

15 Am.Jur. Damages Sec. 19.

An example of the application of this rule in Vermont Courts in a libel case was in the case next cited. Here, the plaintiff, a clergyman, put into evidence the fact that he lost the privilege of half-fare on the railroads as a result of the libel. As the Court stated on Page 520:

> "The natural and probable damage resulting from the wrongful act charged, he is bound to understand, but he is not bound to forecast such damages as are special and result from peculiar and exceptional circumstances."

Shurtleff v. Stevens, 51 Vt. 501—(headnote 2)

III FAILURE OF COURT TO CHARGE AS REQUESTED

A. Similarity of crimes

The defendant requested that the Court charge that if the crime that the plaintiff had in fact committed and the crime published had the same degree of criminality, they (the Jury) should award no damages for that item. The Court refused to do so. (Tr. 71)

Although generally the defendant, to justify, must prove the same crime published, there are exceptions. In some cases, when the crimes were equally serious, the Court has refused to allow damages. Seelman's *The Law of Libel* Page 173 and 304 [a study of New York libel law—Ed.]

In the instant case, both crimes are serious, each having a penalty of not more than $500 and imprisonment up to two years or both, although the minimum fine in the case of driving while under the influence is $50.

B. Jury should have been instructed to consider in mitigation of damage and to rebut malice, that the publication of November 25 charging driving while intoxicated was the result of an inadvertent mistake.

The defendant further requested the Court to charge that if the publication (November 25) was the result of an inadvertent mistake or if there were no malice, they should consider these in mitigation. (Tr. 71)

The Court refused so to charge, and its charge in regard to mitigation was, in substance, that such evidence that would tend toward the truth of the publication should be considered in mitigation. (Tr. 72)

It is submitted that this was error as truth is a defense and a justification and not mitigation. The uncontradicted evidence of Mrs. Benton showed that an inadvertent mistake happened when she misread her notes, misreading D.W.S. (Driving While Under Suspension) for D.W.I. (Driving While Under the Influence). (Tr. 46)

It is a well known principle of law that the Court is required to charge on every material issue in the case and the presence or absence of malice is an appropriate issue. Failure to give an instruction in that regard when requested should warrant a reversal. 33 Am.Jur. Libel and Slander Sec. 304. As to the issue of malice see Hutchinson v. Wheeler, 35 Vt. 330.

In the above case, the Court charged that if the defendant in a defamation case made a mistake, such should be considered in showing lack of malice. The Court stated that the words spoken implied malice, and the defendant might rebut such implication (see Pages 334 and 335 as to Court's charge and 336 as to the ruling).

It is therefore submitted that failure to charge on the issue of malice, and in particular, failure to charge as requested in regard to the mistake of the defendant in mitigation of damages, is reversible error. The Jury could not reach a fair verdict without proper instruction.

IV IT WAS ERROR FOR THE COURT NOT TO SET ASIDE THE VERDICT ON THE GROUND THAT THE DAMAGES WERE EXCESSIVE

Admitting, for the sake of this argument, that all elements of damage were properly in the case, the verdict could not even then be justified.

Here was a young man who was and is a sergeant in the Air Force. He could not prove that the libel hurt his career. The items he offered in damages were his loss of business, about $1500, and his loss on the sale of the house, about $1000. He was transferred to Newfoundland soon after the publication. (Tr. 35)

It is admitted that the only items that were in dispute were the allegations that the plaintiff was dropped from the Patrol for misuse of authority and the admitted error in stating Driving While Intoxicated for Driving While Under Suspension. (Tr. 27 bottom of page and Tr. 28)

None of the proofs showed actual malice; yet the Court charged that "exemplary damages are to be governed wholly by the malice or wantonness of the defendant. . ." (Tr. 69)

If the above is a true statement of law, and the defendant concedes that it is, then the awarding of $1000 above all possible compensatory damages when no malice is shown is excessive. The lower Court should have granted the defendant's motion. Lancour v. Herald and Globe Ass'n, 112 Vt. 471, Para. 5 Page 476.

CONCLUSION

The defendant's position, based on all the claimed errors, namely, the inclusion of hearsay evidence, the exclusion of the defendant's evidence, the curtailing of his right to cross-examine, the failure to charge the Jury in regard to mistake and malice and lack of malice and the failure to set aside the verdict, considered in toto or individually, were reversible error. The defendant respectfully submits that Justice and the law require that the judgment be reversed.

Respectfully submitted,

/signed/

John Mulvey,
Attorney for the defendant

———

Mr. Mulvey's legal arguments utilize Vermont cases and several legal textbooks and encyclopedias. Notice his continual references to the transcript to show the appellate court just where he thinks the trial judge erred. Mr. Mulvey filed several mimeographed copies of the brief with the Vermont Supreme Court and sent one to Mr. Lisman, who then had a limited time to file his answering brief.

Since Mr. Lisman's brief parallels Mr. Mulvey's in form we shall not include it here. His brief attempted to answer each point in turn by citing different parts of the transcript and other prior cases and treatises, or by arguing that the cases cited by Mr. Mulvey did not really support the point being argued. In summary, Mr. Lisman defended the exclusion of the 1941 sentence on the ground that with public reputation at stake, evidence had to be restricted to general aspects of the plaintiff's character that were common knowledge. He confronted Mr. Mulvey's attack on the admission of the letters head on, emphasizing they were admissible as proof of how Sgt. Towle knew why customers were leaving him, although they would have been hearsay if the truth of their contents had been relevant. Mr. Lisman argued that the defendant's challenge to the authenticity of their signatures had not been raised at the trial and came too late.

On the third point, the equal gravity of the DWS and DWI crimes, Mr. Lisman made a dual attack. First he argued that the two crimes were not in fact of equal gravity since the legislature provided additional penalties for second and third offenses for DWI but did not do so for DWS. His second argument on this point relied on the line of cases starting with Torrey v. Field, to the effect that even if the crimes were considered of equal gravity, the plaintiff was still entitled to at least some damages. Since the defendant had argued for "no damages" in such a case, Mr. Lisman contended that the defendant's requested charge to the jury was properly rejected under either theory.

Finally, Mr. Lisman made a dual attack on the defendant's fourth point, that the damages were excessive. He argued first that since the defendant had admitted that $2,500 was reasonable, only $1,000 was in question, and then asserted that malice could be found because the second story did not explicitly retract the first one and instead harshly attacked Sgt. Towle's past and present character. Secondly, even if exemplary damages were unwarranted, the extra $1,000 could be defended as compensatory damages reimbursing Sgt. Towle for his humiliation and general loss of reputation. The brief concluded by urging that the trial court's judgment be affirmed in all respects.

Mr. Mulvey had the opportunity, which he did not use, to file a "reply" brief answering any unexpected arguments in the appellee's brief.

V. THE APPEAL IS DECIDED

After all the briefs have been written the attorneys usually argue the case orally before the justices of the Vermont Supreme Court, unless the parties agree that the appeal presents such a clear-cut question that argument would be superfluous. In the latter instance a decision would be reached solely on the basis of the briefs "submitted."

Before hearing oral argument the justices will usually have read the opposing briefs and given some thought to the case. At the argument the appellant's attorney will briefly summarize what he believes to be the salient facts, and will then make his most important arguments orally. The Vermont Supreme Court permits "not more than one hour" for argument on each side, and the court may shorten even that. This necessitates careful use of one's allotted time. But the attorneys, first the appellant's and then the appellee's, do not make speeches. They expect frequent interruptions by questions from the bench and indeed hope these will occur because they will indicate whatever difficulties an individual justice is having with a specific assertion in the brief or argument. Sometimes these arguments become dry and technical and often the dispute may narrow down to the question of whether a particular word in the judge's charge conveyed the correct impression to the jury. Though there is little of the obvious drama of the trial courtroom, the appellate argument has considerable solemnity and underlying tension.

Sometimes a party who loses at trial is dissatisfied with his attorney and retains someone else for the appeal. Also, some attorneys specialize in trial work while others specialize in appellate practice. We have seen, however, that both Mr. Lisman and Mr. Mulvey were retained for the appeal. The Towle case was argued orally before the Vermont Supreme Court on September 16, 1960. Mr. Mulvey argued for some 40 minutes and then Mr. Lisman took 30 minutes to answer. Oral arguments are rarely transcribed and we do not know what points particularly troubled the five justices. After the argument, the court, as is common, "took the case under advisement" to evaluate the briefs and arguments presented. They may also have undertaken their own legal research and re-read the record. They probably then held a conference to discuss the Towle case and others argued during the same week. At such a conference the justices discuss the merits of the case and each indicates how he expects to vote.

The next decision is whether, in light of the discussion, an opinion should be written in the case. In most systems, the appellate court may decide that the disposition is so clear that an opinion would be superfluous. In these cases the court will only announce its result—"Judgment Affirmed." But in other cases an opinion will be written by a member of the majority, one who is selected either by assignment of the Chief Justice or by some rotation system. That justice must then make an especially close study of the record and briefs to be sure that no subtlety or nuance has escaped the court's attention. He will then draft an opinion containing a brief summary of the facts, his reasons for deciding as he does, and his disposition of the case.

This draft is circulated among his colleagues. If a justice agrees with the result reached in the draft opinion and with its reasons, he will concur in the opinion by signing his name to it. If he agrees with the result reached but not with the reasons given, he may indicate this in one of two ways: he may note simply that he "concurs in the result" or he may write a "concurring opinion" in which he gives different reasons for reaching the same result. If a justice disagrees with the result or disposition contained in the draft opinion, he may indicate this in one of two ways: he may note that he "dissents" from the majority opinion or he may write a "dissenting opinion" to explain his disagreement. "Concurring" and "dissenting" opinions are also circulated to see if other justices find these statements persuasive. Occasionally, justices may change their tentative votes so that what is at first a dissent may become the opinion of the majority.

A majority of the justices need not agree with the proposed opinion, although it *is* necessary for a majority to agree on the disposition. That is, in a three-judge court one justice may vote to affirm the trial court judgment for reason #1, a second justice would also affirm but only for reason #2, and the third justice would reverse. The judgment of the trial court will be affirmed since a majority of the court agreed on that result, even though there was no majority reason.

When all the opinions and votes are final, the decision is ready for announcement. In the Supreme Court of the United States, the announcement of decisions causes great excitement. There is no advance notice of which decisions are ready for announcement. Rather, a justice begins by stating "I have for announcement the opinion and judgment of the court in case No. 159," giving the name and briefly describing the result and reasons that are detailed in his opinion. Other justices who have written separate opinions in the same case will summarize theirs. Copies of all written opinions in the case are then made publicly available. This practice of oral rendition of decisions is rarely followed in state or lower federal courts. Instead, when ready, opinions are merely given to the clerk of the court who notifies the parties, the press and others, of the result and sends them copies of the opinions. The court does not convene formally to announce any decisions.

After pursuing a deliberative process similar to the one outlined above, the Vermont Supreme Court, on November 1, 1960, rendered its decision in the case of Towle v. St. Albans Publishing Co., Inc. and issued the following opinion.

TOWLE v. ST. ALBANS PUBLISHING CO., INC.

SMITH, J. This is an action for libel, brought against the defendant corporation, the owner and publisher of the St. Albans Messenger, a daily newspaper published in St. Albans, Vt. The declaration alleged that on Nov. 25, 1957, the defendant composed and published in the St. Albans Messenger the following article concerning the plaintiff:

"ARRAIGN NINE IN MUNICIPAL COURT

"Ronald Towle of Fairfax, an air policeman, formerly of Enosburg, pleaded guilty to driving while intoxicated.

He paid a fine of $50 and cost of cated. He paid a fine of $50 12.50"

The printing errors shown above appear in the original newspaper article.

The declaration also alleged that on Nov. 26, 1957, the defendant composed and published in the St. Albans Messenger the following article concerning the plaintiff:

"EX-SHERIFFS' PATROLMAN ADMITS COUNT

"A man who five months ago was suspended from the Franklin County Sheriff's Patrol was arraigned in municipal court here yesterday; pleading guilty to driving for the past nine years on a suspended license.

"Ronald Towle, of Fairfax, who was dropped from the patrol in June for 'misuse of authority' was brought before Municipal Court Judge Carl S. Gregg, and was fined $50, plus costs.

"A sergeant with the Air Police at the St. Albans Air Force Base, the 36-year-old native of Enosburg had his license suspended by the commissioner of motor vehicles in 1948, after he failed to file automobile liability insurance while he was overseas in the Army.

"State police said that Towle was convicted of careless and negligent driving, death resulting in St. Albans on May 19, 1941.

"Troopers said a vehicle operated by him was involved in a fatal crash at Bakersfield. A passenger in the car was killed.

"State police said he entered the armed service in 1943, and had his operator's license reinstated in 1946.

"Two years later, troopers said Towle allowed his automobile liability insurance to lapse and his license was again suspended. Police said it has not been reinstated since.

"In court yesterday, the former deputy reported having a Virginia license which is good for 4 years, and expires in 1958. Further, he said his car was fully insured.

"Judge Gregg, meanwhile, said today court records show that as a deputy, the 36-year-old airman was the arresting officer in six motor vehicle cases prosecuted here during the months of May, June and July.

"As a deputy, Towle was given a permit by the commissioner of public safety to equip his car with a siren and red warning lights.

"His appointment as a deputy sheriff was made by Franklin County Sheriff John R. Finn, and was approved by the Attorney-General of Vermont.

"Finn said this morning his commission as deputy and his permit from the department of public safety were withdrawn when he was dropped from the patrol for misuse of authority and on order of the Office of Strategic Information, USAF, Ft. Ethan Allen, Vt."

On November 25, 1957, the plaintiff pleaded guilty to operating a motor vehicle while his right to do so was suspended. The defendant admits that its first news story, quoted above, was in error in stating that the plaintiff pleaded guilty to the charge of "driving while intoxicated." The court below properly charged that this first publication was a libel per se and that under that allegation the defendant was guilty of libel, and defendant took no exception to this part of the charge of the court below.

The defense to the second publication, quoted above, was its truth. The plaintiff, on direct examination, admitted the truth of the second publication except as to that part which stated he had been suspended from the sheriff's patrol for "misuse of authority." Upon this question evidence was presented by both parties.

Jury trial resulted in a verdict for the plaintiff with both compensatory and punitive damages awarded in the one verdict.

The first exceptions briefed by the defendant are to the exclusion of certain evidence by the trial court. It is the contention of the defendant that the sentence received by the plaintiff under the 1941 conviction of careless and negligent driving, death resulting, should have been received in evidence in the case, as well as a certified copy of the court record of the 1941 case, as evidence of the bad character of the plaintiff in the community in mitigation of damages.

It will be remembered that the plaintiff did not dispute the truth of the publication that he had been convicted in 1941. The conviction, in itself, was not disputed, therefore was not in issue, having been admitted. No abuse of discretion is shown in the trial court's exclusion of the certified court record of a conviction already admitted.

The defendant may prove in mitigation of damages the general bad character of the plaintiff in respect to the offense imputed, but he may not prove any particular instances of misconduct unless they are so general that they have affected his general character. Bowen v. Hall, 20 Vt. 232, 241; 35 Am.Jur., Libel and Slander, pp. 205–206.

The matter of the conviction of the plaintiff in 1941 did not come into this case on mitigation of damages, for under the law just quoted it could not. It was in the case only on the issue of the defense of truth in the claimed libel. Just as the specific instance of misconduct was not admissible to mitigate damages in the case, there being no evidence that such instance had affected the general character of the plaintiff, so also the evidence of any penalty received for such misconduct was equally inadmissible. No error is found in the exclusion of this evidence by the trial court.

In order to properly consider the next exceptions taken by the defendant it is necessary to consider some of the evidence in the case relating to the claimed damages suffered by the plaintiff. The plaintiff testified that he had conducted a television and radio repair business from his former home in Fairfax. He further testified that because of the publication in the St. Albans Messenger that he had been convicted of driving while intoxicated he had lost customers of his business, and that because of the ridicule he suffered in Fairfax as a result of the above mentioned publication, he had been obliged to sell his home at a loss and move elsewhere.

Upon cross-examination the defendant questioned the plaintiff as to the effect upon his business of the 1941 conviction, as well as the effect of his conviction on the charge of driving a car while his license was suspended. It was the testimony of the plaintiff that the conviction of 1941, because of its remoteness in time, had no effect upon his business. He also stated that because of letters he had received from former customers, as well as telephone calls, he became informed that the loss of business was due to the publication of the drinking charge. He also testified, without objection, that in talking with these former customers, they informed him that they believed the article in the newspaper, and that they had withdrawn their business from him because of his drinking.

The plaintiff offered in evidence a letter purporting to be from a Mr. Decker, one of his customers, which, in substance, stated that the customer was taking away his business from the plaintiff because of his conviction on the driving while drinking charge. Mr. Decker was not present as a witness in the case, nor was the letter authenticated in any way. It was received in evidence by the trial court over the objection by the defendant that it was hearsay, and that objection is briefed here.

The plaintiff contends that even if the letter was hearsay it was admissible under an exception to the hearsay rule, in that it was admissible, not for the truth of the matters stated therein, but for the purpose of showing the reason for the action of the plaintiff. Yet his actions are not at issue here.

The plaintiff was seeking damages here because of the action of his customers in withdrawing their business. The question presented was the reason for this action of the former customers, and not for any action of the plaintiff himself. On this question the letter was hearsay and should have been excluded.

The plaintiff also, on cross-examination, admitted it was necessary to explain to his friends his conviction on the charge of driving while under suspension. On re-direct examination he testified that upon showing them a letter which he stated he had received from the Commissioner of Motor Vehicles he had no further difficulties with them on that matter. The Commissioner of Motor Vehicles was not a witness in the case, but the court below allowed the alleged letter to be received in evidence over the objection of the defendant that it was hearsay.

The same claim for the admissibility of this letter is made by the plaintiff, that is, that it was properly received for the purpose of showing the reason for the actions of the plaintiff, but again, the reason for the action of the plaintiff was not in issue here. The issue upon which this evidence was received was the reactions of the customers and friends of the plaintiff to his conviction on the charge of driving while his license was suspended, bearing upon the matter of damages. On this matter the letter was hearsay and should have been excluded.

But it is not enough that the defendant show that there was error in the admission of these two letters. The burden is upon him to also show that the admission in error was to his prejudice. The test is whether in the circumstances of the particular case it sufficiently appears that the rights of the complaining party have been injuriously affected by the error. Parker v. Roberts, 99 Vt. 219, 225, 131 A. 21, 49 A.L.R. 1382.

The plaintiff testified, without objection, that he suffered no loss of business because of the conviction of driving while under suspension, basing his answer upon conversations with his customers. He also testified, without objection, that these customers informed him that they were withdrawing their custom because of the erroneous newspaper article of his being convicted of driving while intoxicated. He further testified, again without objection, to the fact that other letters he had received stated that the writers were removing their business because of the drinking charge. This evidence was not controverted. The effect of the two letters, admitted in error, was only cumulative to other admitted evidence in the case to the same point. Being only cumulative to other evidence received we cannot find that it was such error as to injuriously affect the defendant. With the uncontroverted evidence being that the conviction for driving while his license had been suspended had no effect upon the damages suffered by the plaintiff, evidence that, at best, could only go to the seriousness of that conviction, was not prejudicial.

The same holding must be made to the admission of the alleged letter from a customer of the plaintiff withdrawing his business from the plaintiff because of the publication of a conviction of driving while intoxicated against the plaintiff, which was not true. The plaintiff testified, without objection, that he was informed by the customers who withdrew their trade, that it was because of this publication. He further testified, without objection being made, that letters he had received from other customers contained the same reason for withdrawing their custom.

The admission of the letter, which was hearsay and in error, was only cumulative to other uncontroverted evidence in the case not objected to by the defendant. Being only cumulative in effect, we cannot find that it was such error as to injuriously affect the defendant.

The next exception of the defendant for our consideration was to the admission of evidence on the question of damages. It was the testimony of the plaintiff that, as a result of the libel, he was subject to derision and ridicule in Fairfax, where he then lived. He further testified that to get away from this ridicule he sold the house that he then owned in Fairfax at a loss of $1,000.

No objection was made by the defendant when this testimony was introduced. The plaintiff was cross-examined on the matter of the sale of the house by the counsel for the defendant. The first objection made by the defendant to the introduction of the evidence was by a motion to strike such evidence at the time that testimony on both sides of the case had been closed. The rule in Vermont is well established that a party cannot allow testimony to be introduced without objection, thereby waiving his right to object, and then at some subsequent stage of the trial insist on its exclusion. Edmunds Brothers v. Smith, 95 Vt. 396, 401, 115 A. 187, and cases cited therein. The only excuse offered by the defendant for the delay in objecting to the evidence in his motion to the court below was that he had no way of knowing if the evidence objected to would be "tied up" with the issues at the time it came in. It is sufficient to say that defendant could have noted his objection to such evidence, at the time it was first introduced, subject to it being later connected with the issues in the case. No error is found.

The next objection of the defendant is to the charge of the lower court. Defendant excepted to the failure of the lower court to charge that if the jury found that the gravity or criminality of a conviction of driving while intoxicated, which appeared in the erroneous publication by the defendant, was the same as the actual conviction for driving while his license was suspended, then the jury should award no damages. The argument of the defendant would seem to be that a jury should award no damages for a libellous publication of a conviction that had never happened, provided that there has been a conviction of the plaintiff on an offense of similar gravity.

This Court in the early case of Torrey v. Field, 10 Vt. 353, 408, said:

> "The authorities all concur in this, that where the defendant will justify by showing the truth of the matters charged in the libel, it must be the truth of the 'very charge', and it is not sufficient to plead and prove the plaintiff guilty of a similar offense, or even of one more flagrant."

This exception cannot be sustained.

The defendant also excepted to the failure of the lower court to charge that if the publication was the result of an inadvertent mistake, or if there was no malice, the jury should consider these in mitigation of damages. The evidence disclosed that the publication of Nov. 25, 1957, in which it was stated that the plaintiff pleaded guilty to driving while intoxicated, had resulted because the reporter for the defendant publication had misread an abbreviation in the notes she had taken at the municipal court proceeding. Lack of malice may be shown by a defendant for the purpose of mitigating special or punitive damages, but malice, or the lack thereof, is not for the consideration of the jury on compensatory damages. Lancour v. Herald and Globe Ass'n., 112 Vt. 471, 478–480, 28 A.2d 396.

The exception taken by the defendant was the failure to charge that if the publication was an inadvertent mistake, or if there was no malice, they should consider that item in mitigating any damage. But if the lower court had so charged it would have been in error, for the matter of malice was not for the consideration of the jury on compensatory damages. Further, an examination of the charge given by the lower court satisfies us that the jury was charged correctly upon the matter of malice in assessing punitive damages.

The last exception briefed by the defendant is to the denial of the motion of the defendant to set aside the verdict on the ground that the damages were excessive. The motion of the defendant, and the grounds upon which it was based, is not part of the record before us.

This is a question concerning which the appellate court on review has no discretion. The only question here for our determination is whether the trial court abused its discretion. In considering this question, we are bound to indulge every reasonable presumption in favor of the ruling below, bearing in mind that the trial court was in the better position to determine the question. Lancour v. Herald and Globe Ass'n, 112 Vt. 471, 483, 28 A.2d 396; Belock v. State Mut. Fire Ins. Co., 106 Vt. 435, 443, 175 A. 19, 23.

We cannot say, on the record before us, that the trial court exercised its discretion on grounds or for reasons clearly untenable, or to an extent clearly unreasonable, which, in this state, is the recognized test of abuse of discretion. Stone v. Briggs, 112 Vt. 410, 415, 26 A.2d 828.

Judgment affirmed.

Notes and Questions

1. One technical matter may be explored quickly. Most states employ an official court reporter to index and publish the actions taken by the state's supreme court. In Vermont, the reporter printed the Towle opinion in Volume 122 of the Vermont reports at page 134. State practices vary, and these volumes are often quite delayed. In the late 19th century a private company began a service of making all reports of federal appellate and state supreme courts rapidly available. These private state reports are compiled on a regional basis so that the Towle case, for example, is printed in Volume 165 of the Atlantic Reporter, 2nd series, at page 363. Other state court opinions appear in other regional reporters: Northeast, Northwest, Pacific, Southeast, Southern, and Southwest. Cases decided by the United States Courts of Appeals appear only in the "Federal Reporter" and opinions selectively chosen from the federal district courts appear only in the "Federal Supplement". In the Supreme Court of the United States there is an official reporter and his volumes are known as "United States Reports." Two private companies also report Supreme Court opinions.

These reporting methods facilitate legal research and provide convenient short "citations" to all cases. Later when a lawyer wants to refer to the Towle case in a brief he will do so as follows: "Towle v. St. Albans Publishing Co., Inc., 122 Vt. 134, 165 A.2d 363 (1960)" to show the two volumes in which the case may be found and the year in which it was decided. The official citation to the state reporter appears first and the unofficial, regional, citation is listed second.

Federal citations follow this form: "Grant v. Reader's Digest Ass'n, Inc., 151 F.2d 733 (2d Cir. 1945), cert. denied 326 U.S. 797, 66 S.Ct. 492, 90 L.Ed. 485 (1946)." This means that the Grant case was decided by the United States Court of Appeals for the Second Circuit in 1945 in an opinion that may be found in Volume 151 of the Federal Reporter, Second Series, at page 733. The losing party in the Court of Appeals petitioned the Supreme Court of the United States for a writ of certiorari but the writ was denied. This action of the Supreme Court took place in 1946 and is officially reported in Volume 326 of the United States Reports at page 797. It is also reported in Volume 66 of the Supreme Court Reports and Volume 90 of the Lawyer's Edition—both privately published reports of Supreme Court action.

2. We may now return to the opinion itself. Since no dissents or concurrences are indicated, we may conclude that the five justices of the Vermont Supreme Court not only unanimously agreed to "affirm" the trial court's judgment, but also agreed on one opinion. What is the thrust of the opinion? How can the court tell whether the errors were prejudicial? Should the briefs have anticipated this?

3. What does this "affirmance" mean to Sgt. Towle and to the St. Albans Publishing Co? In light of the limited function of appellate review we may reasonably conclude that this affirmance means simply that Judge Hill in his many rulings and orders committed no error that would justify reversal of Sgt. Towle's $3,500 judgment. Indeed, the Towle opinion illuminates the essence of limited appellate review: it reviews only the trial judge's conduct, refrains from "second-guessing" the jury, overlooks what it regards as "harmless" error, (such as the trial court's admission of letters to the plaintiff) and respects the requirement that a litigant raise his objections at the first opportunity in order to preserve the right to complain at a later time.

4. In a case where the reviewing court does find prejudicial error, it will "reverse" the lower court's judgment and will nor-

mally "remand" the case back to the trial court with its mandate, or instructions, directing the subsequent disposition of the case. The precise form of these directions will depend upon what the appellate court actually decided. Thus, if it decided that the appellant was prejudiced by the erroneous admission or exclusion of some evidence, or by erroneous instructions to the jury, it will remand the case with instructions to grant the appellant a new trial. If it decided that the trial court erroneously denied a motion for a directed verdict or judgment n. o. v., it will remand with instructions to the trial court to grant the requested motion and enter judgment accordingly, without the necessity for a new trial on the merits. Since the appellate court in the Towle case found no "prejudicial error" and affirmed the judgment below, the trial court judgment remained in effect.

5. Is the case now finally at an end? Not necessarily. In Vermont as in all legal systems the losing party in the appellate court may seek a "re-hearing" or "re-argument". It is not enough for the losing party to assert its disappointment. One of the obvious but often forgotten aspects of litigation is that roughly half the litigants are ultimately disappointed. Rather, the losing party must convince the court that it has "misapprehended or overlooked some point, whether of law or fact, which was presented in the briefs upon the original argument of the case, and which would probably affect the result." This formulation, fairly typical, is taken from the rules of the Vermont Supreme Court. As the opinion suggests, however, the justices understood the case thoroughly and Mr. Mulvey was unable to find any point coming within the quoted rule and made no motion for a rehearing. If within 15 days after the original decision no rehearing motion is made the decision of the Vermont Supreme Court becomes effective.

As far as Vermont is concerned, the litigation is at an end. In a federal system, however, a single final court must resolve disputes involving federal questions. In the United States, litigants who lose in the highest court of a state may carry their cases to the Supreme Court of the United States. In this sense the Supreme Court is the apex of both the federal and the state court structures, though in this latter instance its jurisdiction is limited to cases involving substantial federal questions. A few such cases must be heard by the Supreme Court but most of them lie in the Court's discretionary jurisdiction. A litigant wishing to invoke this discretion must generally show the Supreme Court that the "state court has decided a federal question of substance not theretofore determined by this court, or has decided it in a way probably not in accord with applicable decisions of this court." The Court's "not in accord" language presumably reflects not concern that a case has been decided incorrectly, but rather that matters involving federal questions be decided uniformly throughout the country.

If the St. Albans Publishing Co. had wanted to seek review by the Supreme Court of the United States, its papers would have been titled "St. Albans Publishing Co. v. Towle" because in some courts, including the Supreme Court, the party seeking review is named first. But in most courts, including the Vermont Supreme Court, the original plaintiff's name always comes first no matter who is seeking review.

In any event, because there was no conceivable federal question in the case, Mr. Mulvey's client sought no further review. Thus, the case was finally concluded.

Can we be assured that the outcome of the Towle case is "correct?" Of course not. We can say that all six of the judges who considered the questions agreed on a resolution but still they all may have been wrong. Remember that the case arose because one party had a grievance against another. The state provided this extensive litigation process in order to resolve that dispute and award whatever remedy, if any, was deemed appropriate. So long as there has been no fraud practiced by the parties, Sgt. Towle's judgment is now irrevocable. It is essential that civil litigation should finally terminate so that the parties may know who was "right" and act accordingly. Here a final and considered termination may be preferable to an unending search for "justice," although in criminal law we think the interest in "justice" outweighs the interest in finality and resolution. Thus, the criminal law provides continual opportunity for a convicted man to argue that there has been a miscarriage of justice.

W. THE CASE CONCLUDES

All efforts to review the merits of the trial court judgment have been either exhausted or waived and that judgment still stands. But in rereading it, you will notice that it does not order the defendant to do anything. The language "plaintiff recover of the defendant" $3,500 is essentially a declaration that on the facts of this case the law entitles the plaintiff to that sum from the defendant. Again we see the passive nature of the process. If plaintiff wishes to collect this judgment he must take further action.

The court's posture is less passive if the plaintiff wants something other than money from the defendant. If he wants the defendant to stop doing something, the plaintiff will seek an "injunction" that "enjoins" the defendant from, for example, continuing to emit noxious smoke from its factory smokestack. In such a case, if the court decides that the plaintiff is entitled to this relief, the court will write its order in language directing the defendant to cease emitting the smoke. If the defendant fails to obey the court order, he will be held in "contempt of court" and punished. In the Towle situation, however, since plaintiff seeks only money, no order directs the defendant to do anything.

No matter what relief the plaintiff is seeking, if the final judgment is for the defendant, the preservation of the status quo requires no further action. If the same plaintiff sues the same defendant again for the same claimed wrong, the defendant need only point to the first judgment to terminate the second case quickly.

If the defendant refuses to honor a judgment against him by voluntary payment the plaintiff can obtain the assistance of the government in enforcing his judgment. On plaintiff's request, the clerk of the court that has rendered the judgment will order the sheriff to seize as much as necessary of the defendant's property within the state and sell it at public auction, satisfying the judgment out of the proceeds and remitting the balance, if any, to the defendant.

Sometimes the sheriff finds it difficult to execute this order. We read often of defendants who attempt to avoid paying judgments by transferring assets to relatives or by moving away. If Mr. Lisman had been concerned about this prospect he would have tried to take steps to be sure that he could collect any judgment he got. Recall that his original papers were entitled "writ of attachment" even though he did not then ask that property be attached. If Mr. Lisman had had any doubts about the defendant's solvency or stability he might actually have "attached" at the outset, which states allow in varying situations. During the course of the litigation the defendant would then, in effect, be unable to sell the "attached" property, though it could probably keep using it. When the case ended the plaintiff would have this property available to insure payment, like collateral on a loan.

If the defendant were to seek refuge in another state, plaintiff could take his judgment to defendant's new state and invoke the "full faith and credit" clause of the Constitution that we discussed earlier in terms of non-resident motorist statutes. But if the defendant runs off to Brazil and leaves no assets here the plaintiff has serious problems. Although the United States has entered into treaties with some other countries to aid citizens in this situation, the process is costly and the defendant may be hard to locate. The general point is clear: Winning a judgment does not insure collecting the money.

Of course, the mere existence of levy and sale procedures for the enforcement of judgments encourages most defendants to satisfy judgments against them voluntarily. On November 16, 1960, after expiration of the rehearing period, Mr. Lisman wrote to Mr. Mulvey requesting the immediate voluntary payment of the $3,500 judgment. Obviously neither party seriously contemplated petition for review by the Supreme Court of the United States. Note that in return for the convenience of the defendant's voluntary compliance with the outstanding judgment, the plaintiff was willing to waive his right to interest and the few costs he could legally claim.

November 16, 1960

John Mulvey, Esq.,
Attorney at Law
St. Albans, Vermont

Dear John:

Re: Towle libel judgment.

As you know, the Supreme Court has now affirmed the judgment in the lower court in favor of the plaintiff. I shall look for your check within the next few days.

I am authorized by my client to state that he will accept the sum of $3,500.00 in satisfaction of the judgment, which will exclude all interest and costs, provided it is paid within the next week or so. However, my client insists that, if payment is delayed beyond that time, I collect the full amount of the judgment, which will include the amount of the verdict, $3,500.00, with interest at the legal rate from the date of judgment, which was October 20, 1959, together with costs, which will be fixed by the Clerk of the Supreme Court and will include the costs of the record, the folio, costs of the briefs, etc.

It is not my intention to be unduly harsh, in this matter but I am, of course, bound by my client's instructions and I do consider that it is only fair that he have his money promptly on the judgment which is now more than one year old.

Very truly yours,
/s/ Louis Lisman

This letter led to an extended series of letters and telephone calls that finally culminated in an exchange of documents in December, 1960. The plaintiff executed a "release" form in which he agreed to "release" all claims he might have against the defendant for libels committed prior to the date of the settlement. In return the defendant forwarded a check for $3,500 made out to both Mr. Lisman and Sgt. Towle to facilitate their fee arrangements. Finally on December 23, when all documents had been exchanged, Mr. Mulvey filed in the county court a "stipulation" signed by both attorneys saying the court records should show "Judgment satisfied" as the final entry in the case. Mr. Mulvey then wrote Mr. Lisman to "feel free to cash the check."

This "stipulation" would prevent any subsequent attempt to enforce the judgment. It constitutes the final step in the litigation process and concludes our study of how the legal system seeks to resolve civil disputes.

X. SOME OBSERVATIONS

Although the litigation process is the most conspicuous aspect of the law and is the sole function of courts, it is not the sole— nor even the dominant—activity of the legal profession. In most instances litigation implies failure; most attorneys "specialize" in trying to avoid lawsuits. A man who wants a will leaving different amounts to different persons at different times expects his lawyer to draft a document that clearly and legally achieves these purposes. The lawyer serves as counsellor in helping the client formulate his wishes and then acts as draftsman in seeking to carry them out. If the lawyer has done his job well, and the affected parties behave rationally, there will be no litigation when the client dies. If a lawsuit does develop, this may suggest that the lawyer has failed to provide for certain contingencies or has used ambiguous language or has not followed the legal requirements for wills.

This example applies to more complex situations as well. Perhaps the most important is the institution of contract negotiations. The attorneys' underlying premise in negotiating such agreements is generally that both parties will gain from a clearly understood and amicable working arrangement. If one party tries to "pull a fast one" the arrangement will collapse, an acrimonious lawsuit will ensue, and the anticipated benefits will never materialize. Where there is strong incentive for the parties not to let a dispute destroy an advantageous long-term arrangement, the contract may provide that if certain types of disagreement arise and cannot be settled the parties will not resort to litigation, but will submit the dispute to arbitration or some other informal method of reaching an accord.

By implication, then, the cases most likely to reach formal litigation are those in which the parties have had no prior relationship. This is characteristic of much of tort law and criminal law, which do comprise the major burden on the courts. Tort law involves such cases as automobile accidents and defamation, where the parties are usually brought together for the first time by the particular incident that creates the controversy. In this situation three basic factors contribute to the likelihood of litigation. First, the incident has caused harm to someone who is therefore antagonistic. Second, the facts giving rise to the harm are often more sharply in dispute, as is the applicable rule of law. (In contract cases the relevant rules of law may be agreed upon in the initial agreement.) Third, no generally beneficial long-term working relationship exists to provide an incentive for settlement.

Tort law and criminal law account for most litigation, but even in these areas the "settlement" rate is high. Although at least 95% of all automobile cases are settled either without formal litigation or in the very early litigation stages, so many accidents occur that even a load of one in 20 cases causes judicial strain. In criminal law the court is involved in sentencing the well over 75% of all defendants who "settle" their cases by pleading guilty either to the offense charged or to a lesser offense, as well as in conducting trials of the remainder.

The settlement process is often further encouraged by the large sums in dispute. Uncertainty about how the jury will view the facts, as seen in Towle, and how the judge will apply the law makes parties wary of risking an all or nothing result. Is this type of compromise socially desirable? After all, one of the parties is correct and would be vindicated by the court if he persevered. In this view, do compromises undercut the pursuit of justice? Does our law ever forbid compromises?

In what ways has this "biography" affected your attitude toward the law? How about your attitude toward the role of the lawyer? Does the adversary system trouble you? How do you feel now about lawyers' accepting unpopular cases? Do you think, seeing how the law functions at a fairly elementary level, that legal services should be made available to all citizens?

Has your attitude toward the role of the jury changed? Do you think that the jury advances the primary goals of the legal system, or does it impede them? Under what circumstances would you prefer a trial before a jury?

Is the concept of "justice" adequately served by the system just described? Are you surprised that this system works as well as it does? What do you consider to be its major flaws?

These are just a few of the many questions that the foregoing study was designed to provoke. Such issues are basic to the vitality of the American legal system, and deserve the interest of every citizen.

*

AUTHORS' BIOGRAPHIES

FRANK, Jerome N. (1889–1957). Judge, U. S. Court of Appeals, Second Circuit, 1941–57. Practiced law in Chicago and New York, 1912–33; general counsel, Agricultural Adjustment Administration and Federal Surplus Relief Corporation, 1933–35; Commissioner, Securities and Exchange Commission, 1937–41, Chairman, 1939–41; visiting lecturer in law, Yale University Law School, 1946–57. Author, Law and the Modern Mind (1930), If Men Were Angels (1942), Fate and Freedom (1945), Courts on Trial (1949), and others.

JAMES, Fleming, Jr. Born 1904. Professor of Law. At Yale University since 1933. Practiced law in New Haven, 1928–33; Director of Litigation Division, Office of Price Administration, 1943–45. Editor, with Thurman Arnold, Cases on Trials, Judgments and Appeals (1936); with Harry Shulman, Cases and Materials on Torts (2d ed. 1952). Author, Civil Procedure (1965); with Fowler Harper, Law of Torts (1956).

KALVEN, Harry, Jr. Born 1914. Professor of Law. At University of Chicago since 1945. Practiced law in Chicago 1939–42. Director, Chicago Jury Project. Author, with Walter Blum, The Uneasy Case for Progressive Taxation (1953); with Zeisel and Buchholz, Delay in the Court, (1959); with Charles Gregory, Cases and Materials in Torts (1959); with Walter Blum, Public Law Perspectives on a Private Law Problem (1965); and The Negro and the First Amendment (1965).

ROSTOW, Eugene V. Born 1913. Under Secretary for Political Affairs, U. S. State Department, since 1967; Professor, 1938–67, and Dean, 1955–65, Yale Law School. Author, A National Policy for the Oil Industry (1948), Planning for Freedom (1959), and The Sovereign Prerogative (1962).

APPENDIX II

NOTES FOR FURTHER READING

Readers who wish to learn more about our legal system may find the following reading list helpful. Titles available in paperback are preceded by an asterisk (*).

A. **The American Legal System—An Overview**

Farnsworth, E. Allan, An Introduction to the Legal System of the United States (1963).

Karlen, Delmar, Law in Action (1964).

* Mayers, Lewis, The Machinery of Justice: an Introduction to Legal Structure and Process (1963).

Mayers, Lewis, The American Legal System: The Administration of Justice in the United States by Judicial, Administrative, Military and Arbitral Tribunals (1964).

B. **Other Legal Systems**

* Abraham, Henry J., The Judicial Process: An Introductory Analysis of the Courts of the United States, England, and France (1962).

* Bedford, Sybille, The Faces of Justice: A Traveller's Report (1961).

* Berman, Harold, Justice in the U.S.S.R.: An Interpretation of Soviet Law (1963).

Bohannan, Paul, Justice and Judgment Among the Tiv (1957).

Cohen, Jerome, Criminal Process in the People's Republic of China: An Introduction, 79 Harvard Law Review 469 (1966).

Cowen, Zelman, Legal and Cultural Changes in China (1962).

* Feifer, George, Justice in Moscow (1964).

Gibbs, James L., Jr., Poro Values and Courtroom Procedure in a Kpelle Chiefdom, 18 Southwestern Journal of Anthropology 341 (1962).

Gluckman, Max, The Judicial Process Among the Barotse of Northern Rhodesia (1955).

Hoebel, E. Adamson, The Law of Primitive Man (1954).

Hogbin, Herbert Ian, Law and Order in Polynesia: A Study of Primitive Legal Institutions (1961).

194

Llewellyn, Karl and Hoebel, E. Adamson, The Cheyenne Way: Conflict and Case Law in Primitive Jurisprudence (1941).

C. Law and Society

Cohen, Morris R., Law and the Social Order (1933).

Davis, F. James, and others, Society and the Law: New Meanings for an Old Profession (1962).

Ehrlich, Eugen, Fundamental Principles of the Sociology of Law (1962 ed.).

Eiseley, Loren C. and others, ed., Social Control in a Free Society (1960).

Evan, William M., ed., Law and Sociology (1962).

Kelsen, Hans, Law as a Specific Social Technique, 9 University of Chicago Law Review 75 (1941).

Pound, Roscoe, Social Control Through Law (1942).

Pound, Roscoe, Law and Morals (1923).

D. American Legal Procedure

* Botein, Bernard and Gordon, Murray A., The Trial of the Future: Challenge to the Law (1963).

* Chodorov, Stephan, A Criminal Case (1964).

Kalven, Harry, Jr. and Zeisel, Hans, The American Jury (1966).

Karlen, Delmar, Primer of Procedure (1950).

* Karlen, Delmar, The Citizen in Court: Litigant, Witness, Juror, Judge (1964).

* Lewis, Anthony, Gideon's Trumpet (1964). A description of the events leading to Gideon v. Wainwright, the case in which the Supreme Court required states to provide counsel in all felony cases.

* Peck, David, The Greer Case, A True Court Drama (1955).

* Taper, Bernard, Gomillion versus Lightfoot (1962). An account of a Supreme Court case involving a state's efforts to disenfranchise some Negro voters.

* Westin, Alan F., The Anatomy of a Constitutional Law Case: Youngstown Sheet and Tube Co. v. Sawyer; the Steel Seizure Decision (1958).

E. The American Legal Profession

Barrett, Edward F., The Adversary System and Ethics of Advocacy, 37 Notre Dame Lawyer 479 (1962).

Countryman, Vern and Finman, Ted, The Lawyer in Modern Society (1966).

Curtis, Charles P., The Ethics of Advocacy, 4 Stanford Law Review 3 (1951).

* Eulau, Heinz and Sprague, John D., Lawyers in Politics, a Study in Professional Convergence (1964).

Griswold, Erwin N., Law and Lawyers in the United States: the Common Law under Stress (1964).

Horsky, Charles, The Washington Lawyer (1952).

Mayer, Martin, The Lawyers (1967).

Porter, Charles O. and Blaustein, Albert P., The American Lawyer: a Summary of the Survey of the Legal Profession (1954).

Pound, Roscoe, The Lawyer from Antiquity to Modern Times (1953).

Smigel, Erwin O., The Wall Street Lawyer: Professional Organization Man? (1964).

F. Novels About Law and Lawyers

* Cozzens, James, The Just and the Unjust (1942).

* Dickens, Charles, Bleak House (1852).

Kafka, Franz, The Trial (1937).

* Traver, R., Anatomy of a Murder (1958).

Trollope, Anthony, Orley Farm (1862).

G. Actual Defamation and Privacy Cases

* Dean, Joseph, Hatred, Ridicule or Contempt: A Book of Libel Cases (1953).

Ernst, Morris L. and Lindey, Alexander, Hold Your Tongue! Adventures in Libel and Slander (1932).

Ernst, Morris L. and Schwartz, Alan U., Privacy: The Right to be Let Alone (1962).

* Gavin, Clark, Famous Libel and Slander Cases of History (1962).

* Nizer, Louis, My Life in Court (1961). Including an account of the famous libel case brought by Quentin Reynolds against Westbrook Pegler.

* Nizer, Louis, The Jury Returns (1966). Including an account of the suit by John Henry Faulk against Aware, Inc., for its practice of "blacklisting" in the entertainment industry.

†